T0163212

# THE
# CAMINO

# THE CAMINO

## A SINNER'S GUIDE

# EDDIE ROCK

BEAUFORT
BOOKS

# THE CAMIN●

ISBN:9780825308819
ebook ISBN: 9780825307690

Library of Congress Cataloging-in-Publication Data on file.

For inquiries about volume orders, please contact:
Beaufort Books
27 West 20th Street, Suite 1102
New York, NY 10011
sales@beaufortbooks.com

Published in the United States by Beaufort Books
www.beaufortbooks.com

Distributed by Midpoint Trade Books
www.midpointtrade.com

Printed in the United States of America

Book Designed by Mark Karis

## "HE WHO WOULD VALIANT BE"

*He who would Valiant be, 'gainst all disaster*
*Let him in constancy follow the Master*
*There's no discouragement shall make him once relent*
*His first avowed intent to be a pilgrim.*
*Who so beset him round with dismal stories*
*Do but themselves confound his strength the more is.*
*No foes shall stay his might, though he with giants fight.*
*He will make good his right to be a pilgrim*
*Since, Lord, thou dost defend us with thy spirit,*
*We know we at the end, shall life inherit.*
*Then fancies flee away! I'll fear not what men say.*
*I'll labour night and day to be a pilgrim.*

—JOHN BUNYAN, *The Pilgrim's Progress*, 1684

*I remember this hymn from Alkborough junior school, 1984.*
—EDDIE ROCK

# CONTENTS

# DEFINITIONS

**sin**
To sin against the church or family, to do wrong, commit a crime, misbehave, transgress, go astray, to fall from grace.

THE SEVEN DEADLY SINS:
*Pride*
*Covetousness*
*Lust*
*Envy*
*Greed*
*Anger*
*Sloth*

*"Let he who is without sin throw the first stone."*
—THE BOOK OF JOHN, CHAPTER EIGHT

**Craic**
an Irish term for having fun

# SUZIE

"HER EYES THEY SHONE LIKE DIAMONDS. I thought her the queen of the land. And her hair hung over her shoulders tied up with a black velvet band."

Well, that's Suzie, almost. . . .

The musicians play on with the traditional old classic, and I sink deeper into the frolicking blue eyes of the mysterious blonde hippie girl sitting beside me. Her happy face sparkles as she giggles naughtily at my tales of global misadventure, and now seems like a good time to introduce Suzie to a very good friend of mine—a special friend who had traveled back from Amsterdam with me (in my boot).

"Mr. Jack Herer?"

As we walk out through the smoky bar to meet Jack, I can't help but notice Suzie's fine physique. Her figure is perfect as far as

I can tell—slim and shapely in all the right places, and when she walks, she takes very long strides, giving her a panther-like step.

"So, where's this Jack friend of yours?" she asks.

"He's just arrived," I say, laughing, then pull a large joint from my pocket. "Ladies before gentlemen," I add, handing her the reefer.

Our hands touch for the first time, releasing a spark of sexual energy that bounces around my body, arousing the basest of intentions.

In the darkness her pretty face glows as she takes a hit, with smoke billowing from her sexy lips into the warm summer night.

"Wow, holy Jeysus." She laughs. "My head's fecking spinning!"

"No—holy Jack Herer, three-time Cannabis Cup winner," I tell her.

"It's similar to the grass we smoked in Spain last year," she says. "You ever heard of the Camino de Santiago?"

"No, I never smoked it!"

"Nooo, you fecking eejit. It's an old pilgrimage route through Spain. I walked it last year with my three girlfriends, Marie, Siobhan, and Clare. Great craic we had every day and plenty of smoke."

As Jack Herer begins to take us on his journey, Suzie begins to take me on hers. I sit back and listen intently as her gorgeous Irish accent spirits me up and away on her fun-filled journey through Spain.

Her happy hippie tale starts in the French Pyrenees and ends five hundred miles later on the Atlantic coast. It sounds like a fantastic adventure, and in my Herered haze I see myself on the trail, becoming one with nature, surrounded by a posse of sexy hippie girls while sleeping out under the stars and having little parties around the campfire, leaving the rat race far behind.

The more I smoke the better it all sounds, and I particularly like the parts of the story where the girls got naked, drunk, or stoned and often all three at the same time.

An alternative hippie holiday, just the job for a tortured soul like me.

"Suzie, I'm sold. How do I get there?"

"Hang on," she says. "When you finish the pilgrimage at the cathedral in Santiago, you put your hand inside a handy hand-shaped hole in a magic pillar worn away by millions of pilgrims' hands and all your worldly sins are forgiven."

"What, all of them?"

"Yeah, all of them," she says.

"What, by putting your hand in a handy hole-shaped handhole?"

"Yeah." She laughs. "And when you get to the sea you burn all of your clothes on the beach, get naked, and party like it's 1999!"

"Wow, I wish I'd been at that one," I tell her.

"Jesus, you should go. It would do you a world of good," she says, smoking the last of the joint.

The moon appears from behind the clouds, and a million tiny sparkles illuminate the darkness.

"We're all made of stars, you know," she says, staring into the night sky longingly.

"Fancy another pint then?" I ask her.

"Jesus. Why not? Sure, we're all sinners after all." She laughs, leading me back inside the swaying pub to the tune of "The Wild Rover."

\* \* \* \*

I wake at the next lunchtime seeing stars, with an epic hangover raging through my shrunken brain. Flashbacks of the previous night keep coming in waves and bounds like some kind of Irish Quentin Tarantino movie with plenty of *Pulp Fiction* and Jack Herer thrown in for good measure. I reach for my Guinness-soaked cigarettes and spy some drunken scribble on the packet. I vaguely remember Suzie writing it—something about some hippie book or something that I should read by some Brazilian guru, but I can hardly make out the words. . . .

Pablo Coolio . . . ? Surely not?

Sounds more like a gangster than a guru.

# THE Z●●

**QUESTION: WHY ARE PIRATES CALLED PIRATES?**

IT'S MINUS FFFECKING FORTY-FFFECKING-SEVEN! The flashing sign outside the hotel says so and the carrion crow on the nearby lamppost squawks a dark reminder of fate, should your luck run out in this arctic wilderness. Two weeks I've been here waiting to get a job on the oilfield, and every day I've trudged to the office, freezing my pips off, and they tell me the same thing: "Come back tomorrow." I mustn't grumble, but it's no wonder they nickname this place "the Zoo." I've met some real animals so far, such as the cocaine-injecting ice truckers, the First Nations Elvis impersonators, and last but not least a bunch of landlocked pirates from Newfoundland. The Newfies, as they are fondly known, all talk like salty sea dogs and introduce themselves in medieval voices, saying, "I be Ron Flynn" and "I be from Newfoundland." They all say "Arrr" a lot, drink a lot, and smoke a lot of weed. But they are a good craic and sound fellas, even the one with no teeth who wears his Wellingtons in the disco.

Apart from all that, being here is no joke, as most days I've been confined to my room. Hibernating like a grizzly bear and achieving a monumental thirty-two-hour snooze marathon, missing a whole day of my life. In my hours of infinite boredom I've been learning to play an antique harmonica, kindly given to me by a drunken Father Christmas impersonator in a biker bar. But after a week I've totally given up due to the mesmerizing effects of BC bud, British Columbia's finest marijuana. . . . As I head down to the bar, the unmistakable green smog of BC comes from under every door in almost every room, with it the familiar clink of beer bottles, pirates' laughter, and *Beavis and Butt-Head* on MTV. One of the drunken pirates walks out of his room wearing only women's underwear and a trucker's cap perched on top of his head.

He sees me and leaps back into the room, screaming like a girl, and pirate laughter echoes down the corridor.

"Haargh haargh haargh, me hearties." They all laugh.

"She won't want them for Christmas now, boy," cackles Long John.

"Aaargh, Jim lad," says Redbeard.

"They be soiled goods now," laughs Blackbeard.

As I walk past their door, they all wail and shout at me to join them in their little world of pirate lunacy, but I make my excuses and hit the bar.

One hundred dollars left and I lose forty-five of it on the poker machine while praying for a gambling miracle to get me out of this arctic nightmare.

So homesick and depressed, I retire back to my dingy room with a big bag of BC and a crate of beer from the bar.

The Christmas television is a total joke. Bruce Springsteen got that right. "Fifty-seven channels and nothing on." Nothing at all to give you the slightest inkling that it's Christmas day on this frozen planet.

After a few puffs of the legendary BC, I'm welded to the mattress, unable to move anything except for my eyes and the remote control. I can't believe American television is such fucking garbage. It's no wonder some of them get so fat and fucked up and go around shooting each other. Maybe if they had better television they would stay indoors and behave. Who knows?

"Next on Discovery, *Ancient Prophecies*. A two-hour Apocalypse Christmas special with your host, David McCallum."

"No fucking way!" I press the remote like a madman.

Anything remotely festive will do—a nice old movie perhaps, or Christmas *Top of the Pops*. Christmas carols, Santa, reindeer—anything! But after another fifty-seven flicks on the remote and eleven pulls on the joint, I'm back with McCallum, Nostradamus, and Old Mother Shipton.

"Jesus Christ! Doom, doom, fucking doom, for fuck's sake."

I chance yet another quick flick through fifty-seven channels of adverts and bullshit and back to where I started.

"Nice one. Apocalypse it is then."

So I smoke my way to oblivion as the BC kicks in a gear and David takes us back through time, with his monotone haunting voice creating the perfect chilling atmosphere for total world destruction.

We begin in the Garden of Eden, with Adam and Eve, the serpent, and the apple and then move on to Noah's Ark, the Great Flood, and how this could all happen again quite soon.

"Great!"

Next we travel to ancient Egypt for a lesson in pyramid alignment, then a short trip to ancient Israel to read the Dead Sea Scrolls as I smoke more and watch with fear and fascination. Then David reads passages from the book of Revelations, writing down the number of the beast, 666, on a blackboard in the studio, and as we come to the end of the show, he adds up all the dates and numbers and then multiplies them with some Egyptian hieroglyphics and calmly announces that the world's gonna end on New Year's Day 2002!

"Fan-fucking-tastic!" Apocalypse just around the corner and here I am in Grimshaw, Alberta, freezing me tits off.

I should be in Ibiza or somewhere, surrounded by scantily clad party girls instead of scantily clad pirates high on cocaine. . . . There's a knock at the door. It's Fat Luke, one of the young pirates.

"Did you know the world is going to end in 2002?" I ask him as he comes in and slumps down on the bed next to me, a little too close for comfort. He shrugs his opinion and flicks the remote to the music video channel. As Kiss take to the stage at Donington Rock Festival 1994, Luke starts talking about his girlfriend back in Newfoundland and the numerous unsavory and probably illegal sex acts he performs with her. I cringe in disgust as he laughs with a mouth like a burned-out fuse box, and I wonder how the fuck someone like him can possibly have a girlfriend. But then again I've seen a bearded abominable snowwoman on a bus in Winnipeg , so it's quite possible. He then starts asking me about my own sexual history, so I quickly change the subject back to heavy metal and pass him the joint as he plays air guitar from the edge of my bed. He's headbanging and frothing at the mouth like a rabid dog, spewing question after question after question. Do I like Slayer, do I like Metallica, Anthrax, and AC/DC?

"Yes, yes, yes," I keep saying.

Now Beavis and Butt-Head are on the screen and he's doing really bad impressions of them while theatrically smoking my joint, then handing it back all bum sucked from his dribbling mouth!

*Why me, Lord?* I think to myself. *Why me?*

I wish he would fuck off and die or leave me alone at least, but it is Christmas after all, so maybe I should try to get into the spirit of things—goodwill to all men and all that bollocks!

"So who's your favorite band than, Luke?" I smile, passing him a beer.

"Anything Satanic." He grins, flicking his tongue between his fingers like Gene Simmons on the telly.

"OK then."

We clink bottles and pull a Christmas cracker.

Luke gets the yellow paper hat, which he puts on his head, making him look even more foolish, and I get the plastic whistle and read out the crap Xmas joke.

*So why are pirates called pirates?*
*Because they arrrrrr!*

## APOCALYPSE NO

WHAT BETTER PLACE TO be on the eve of destruction than back in the Dutch debauchery capital, Amsterdam. I've been partying hard for three weeks now and am still going strong as we build up to the grand finale.

Where's David McCallum? I laugh to myself. He's probably in a reinforced concrete bunker with a big bag of super skunk, stuffing his fat face with popcorn, watching Sky News and waiting.

Last week I had a dream that the Day of Judgment was upon us and the streets of Amsterdam were ablaze, with its famous buildings crumbling into the Damrak. So I took this as a sure sign of impending doom. So with this in mind I sold my car, my bike, and all my joinery tools. Thus giving me plenty of spending money for my final days on planet earth. To ease my transition to the afterlife I have heavily increased my usual intake of powder, pill, and potion in readiness for the final curtain and my descent into hell.

As midnight approaches, I imagine the Four Horsemen of the Apocalypse on the piss around Amsterdam's red light district with their satanic steeds, high on ketamine and laying waste to this modern-day Sodom and Gomorrah.

Stupidly enough, the last memory I have of any sort of destruction is that of a heavily tattooed biker chick shoving a sour-tasting tablet into my mouth, washed down with two large shots of absinthe.

**\* \* \* \***

I always imagined hell to be a hot place for some reason, but I mysteriously find myself frozen to a wooden bench next to the duck pond in Vondelpark, clutching a snorkel tube and wearing a pair of 3-D glasses. What the fuck happened? I check my phone: thirty-two missed calls, fifteen messages, Jan. 02, 2003. McCallum got it wrong.

**\* \* \* \***

A tram bell rings loudly as a barge passes slowly down the old canal, and I make my way home with an epic hangover but very much alive as another winter's day in Holland enfolds. I stop by the old café for a few well-needed hair of the drowned dog lagers and spot McCallum on the large plasma screen wearing a robe and sandals in some kind of Bible film. *"Godverdommer,"* I swear in Dutch. Even with the bad German dubbing, I still get the gist of the story. He's Judas. The betrayer. Paid thirty pieces of silver for betraying poor-old Jesus and betraying me for that matter with his apocalyptic fucking bullshit.

I can't help but watch as he throws the coins into the fire and dives in after them. Big Ronald the barman, shakes his head, cursing, and switches quickly over to the Embassy World Darts at Frimley Green. As Raymond van Barneveld scores a 180, the crowd goes wild and I smile to myself, looking forward to a whole new lease on life.

# SCUNTHORPE

URBAN LEGEND SAYS that an illicit union between a prostitute from Hull and a circus troop from Grimsby produced Scunthorpe's first citizens first recorded in 1354. In modern day the town center can often resemble a cross between Michael jackons *Thriller* video and *Trainspotting*. Immigrants arriving from war torn countries such as Syria and Bosnia often ask, *"What the hell happened here?"*

*"Keep off the grass"* signs adorn most green areas. Not however to protect the grass but to prevent you slipping in dog shit and falling onto discarded drug syringes.

Scunthorpe Backpacker blogger Salvador (Bugsy) Malone says this about his home town on his return in 2014:

*The place now resembled Zagreb or worse. I saw one of my former school friends standing on a corner selling herself to buy drugs and the boy who used to deliver our newspaper was sat begging outside a kebab shop whilst continually scratching his scabby arms.* "Hey Sally mate" *he shouted* "Can you lend us a tenner for old times sake?"

* * * *

So, with the Apocalypse well and truly over, my sorry little tale had to end somewhere, and here I am in hell back in my hometown of Scunthorpe, with no wheels, no job, and no life. As the rain comes down, I dive into the electrical store and spot McCallum on every single television screen in the place. "Bloody hell." I can't believe it. I can't get away from him. Seeing him again only makes me more depressed and angry as he plays some kind of mad scientist on an American police drama.

"*The Great Escape* will never be the same again. Thanks a lot, McCallum, you moron."

"Can I help you with anything, sir?" asks the spotty clerk.

"Yes, do you sell time machines?"

"Erm . . ." He even thinks about it for a moment as I turn to leave.

Back out in the streets my puzzled thoughts debate the concepts of life and religion and how the good citizens of Scunthorpe fit into that equation. If God really did create us in his own image, then I would strongly advise him to lay off the cheap booze, turn off the chip pan, and quit staring into those crazy fairground mirrors. I'd always wanted to get my name in the papers someday, but drunken three-wheeled stunt driving is perhaps not the best way to let off steam. Neither is urinating your name and skillfully managing to dot the *i* of Eddie in the middle of the road outside

Scunthorpe's infamous Blarney stone nightclub, while being cheered on by the queue. Neither was threatening doormen with a stolen antique pistol and whistling the theme tune to *Laurel and Hardy* while being pinned up against a wall by three angry policemen. A good night in the cells is just what you need to bring you back to earth, and a week later on page three of Scunthorpe's *Evening Telegraph*, the quality headline:

"Man Runs into Chip Shop to Avoid Police"

Followed by nearly half a page chronicling my recent ill behaviors. And my subsequent appearance before the magistrate.

However, the best way I find of dealing with complex issues of the law is to pack up your troubles in your old kit bag and smile, smile, smile all the way to the nearest point of departure. But to where?

My friend Steve has said I can go and work for him in the USA, renovating houses in San Francisco. So I suppose it's an option.

Or maybe I could visit Johnny R in Seattle?

Failing that, I can always go back to Holland and work as a carpenter again. But either way I gotta get out of this situation somehow!

In bed that night I dream about my old hippie friend Suzie dressed as a leather-clad vixen, flexing a riding crop and telling me I've been a very bad boy again and how she's going to correct me! With the crack of the whip, her skimpy leather panties hit the floor . . . but what the hell . . . ? My mobile phone is ringing as total darkness descends and I'm awake back in my own bedroom with Suzie long gone.

"And who the fuck is that ruining my fucking dream?"

Missed call: Waz.

\* \* \* \*

With Suzie still fresh in my mind, I head directly for Scunthorpe library.

"Aye up, have you got any books on that walk in Spain?" I ask the dour librarian.

"Which one?" she grunts.

"The Cameo San Diego, I think it's called?"

She spends an age gawping into the computer, and I wonder why I seem to have a knack for rubbing these fuzzy-felt-loving bookworms up the wrong way. Silently she directs me over to the travel section and then disappears in a cloud of dust.

One book is about a pilgrimage, but I'd always thought pilgrims were those God-bothering folk who set sail to America in the sixteenth century. The Pilgrim Fathers, or Christian Brothers, or whatever they were called, dressed in black and white with those silly hats with buckles and square shoes and all that shit. But at last I find a Spanish travel guide with a map of Spain and the Camino de Santiago.

Now, according to this guidebook, I start at a place called Saint-Jean-Pied-de-Port in the French Pyrenees, then head down into the city of Pamplona and walk five hundred miles across Spain to a place called Santiago de Compostela and have all my sins forgiven by putting my hands in the special sin elimination handy hand-hole in the cathedral.

I flick back to the Pamplona section, with photographs of the San Fermín festival and numerous pictures of the running of the bulls down the narrow streets. A few of the pictures are quite disturbing. One man has a bull's horn stuck through his cheek and another has a horn stuck through his leg.

*The running of the bulls often results in the death and serious injury for many participants.*

"Think I'll give that a miss then!"

On my way out I pick up a well-worn copy of *Bravo Two Zero* by SAS action man Andy McNab and a copy of *As I Walked Out One Midsummer Morning* by Laurie Lee, for 50pence each. "Bargain!"

Back out in the streets the aroma of chip-pan impregnated fabrics and cheap tobacco fills the Scunthorpe air, and an unemployed scumbag wearing a dirty tracksuit adds to the ambiance by loudly announcing to his equally scummy friends, "I'm just off to McDonald's for a shit!"

The Basques have got it right, I reckon. Running savage bulls with sharp horns down your local high street is a brilliant idea, especially on benefits day in Scunthorpe without warning. I would love to be the man in charge of opening the barn doors. I notice more groups of track-suited douchebags prowling outside the benefit office and pound shops—swearing, spitting, and shouting while viewing the world with utter contempt through their wicked little reptile eyes set deep in rodent-like faces with miniature spitting clones of themselves gathered at their feet, screaming for Evo-Stik or heroin or whatever they were weaned on. Why they tuck their tracksuits into their socks is a mystery to me. They look like unhealthy spotty gray-faced baseball players, only in this case the ball will have been replaced by a cat or hedgehog wrapped in gaffer tape, a dog with fireworks nailed to its tail, or in most cases a human head.

* * * *

Rows of badly parked Motability scooters clutter the pavement outside the cheap bars, and at ten past ten on this cold morning some good citizens are settling in to their second pint of Nelson Mandela premium-strength Belgium lager. One of them I recognize as Big Jase, an old school friend. He sees me passing and shouts me in for a few beers.

We discuss numerous topical Scunthorpe subjects, such as money or the lack of, recent violence, who's beaten up who, who's fucked who, alcohol abuse, and exchange ideas for getting out of this grim town. We chuckle away the morning while enjoying several pints of quality Export Lager, observing the interesting diversity of North Lincolnshire, so interesting in fact that a couple of old ladies we know actually come to Scunthorpe just to take the piss out of its unfortunate citizens, often stalking their victims up and down the high street while giggling along behind them like drunken schoolgirls.

"Dog the Bounty Hunter, look!" Jase points, laughing his head off.

Through the dirty window we see a strange person struggling to light a Superking cigarette in the fierce wind. It's hard to tell if it's a man or a woman, but either way it's the same face and hairstyle as Dog the Bounty Hunter.

"Great doppelganger," I tell him.

Jase looks at his watch and scoops the last of his pint and then he's off to God knows where, so I finish my drink and leave.

\* \* \* \*

At the zebra crossing on the high street a learner driver screeches to a halt, almost flattening a group of asylum seekers, and now the hooter is beeping loudly with Big Jase leaning out the window, shouting abuse and waving a big tattooed arm at the frightened foreigners as his comb-over-hairstyled driving instructor sits beside him in a state of terror.

A lot of famous people came from Scunthorpe they say.

Tony Jacklin, the golfer, for instance. Bond villain Donald Pleasence; Ian Botham, the cricketer; Graham Taylor, the useless England football manager; and even a member of the Royle family, Nana Royle. Played by actress Liz Smith.

The fact that none of these people ever chose to stay in Scunthorpe is irrelevant.

My mobile is ringing. . . .

"AMSTERDAM," says the excited voice.

AMSTERDAM

## CITY OF SIN

IN HINDSIGHT maybe I should have spent the weeks prior to my epic quest studying maps and learning some useful Spanish phrases, maybe a few long walks in the woods or in the hills with that behemoth of a pack on my back. But instead I spent my time wisely in the local pubs with Laurie Lee and Andy McNab.

Why waste valuable energy is my theory!

Ironically, while I prepared to be a pilgrim, my friend Lindsey Pilgrim (actual name) was, in fact, preparing to be Lindsey Knowles, and I had agreed to go on her stag weekend to Amsterdam. Thus killing two birds with one stone by wearing in my new boots while window-shopping in the red-light district.

* * * *

I check my pack, then check again, making sure I don't forget anything important.

Checklist:

A light-summer shower-proof jacket. After all, I doubt I will hardly wear it, as it's bound to be boiling hot over there.

A small tent.

A self-inflating roll mat.

Two British Army ration packs.

A small camping stove and cooking pots.

Two pairs of jeans.

Five T-shirts.

Two pairs of shorts.

Seven pairs of underpants.

Seven pairs of socks.

A first-aid kit.

A roll of toilet paper.

A luxury Egyptian cotton bath towel.

Aftershave.

A Frisbee.

A travel washing line.

A head torch.

A Swiss Army knife.

A sun hat.

A fold-up chair.

Two plastic water bottles.

A travel pillow.

A cheap yellow poncho.

One pair of earplugs.

A large box of condoms.

A map of Spain.
A day pack.
A Spanish phrase book.
A harmonica.
Sun cream.
Sunglasses.
A shaving kit.
*Bravo Two Zero*.
Laurie Lee book.
£3,000 bank loan.

Last but not least, my Franklin W7 Euro Translator (every budding Bond should have one).

## BON VOYAGE!

Amsterdam has all you can ask for when it comes to sins of the flesh. The new boots are wearing in well, pacing up and down the various seedy alleys, and all this window-shopping has worked up a hearty thirst for strong lager, so we all pile into the Old Sailor in the very heart of the red-light area.

Luckily we get window seats across from the prostitutes and play our silly game, Whores and Jockeys, a gambling game invented by Waz, where we bet on how long we think the rider (punter) will stay in the saddle (whore), with Waz commentating on the probable or improbable action behind the curtain, with hilarious results.

Our friend Jay wins today's money with a straight-in-and-out fifty-four seconds. Crack whore versus puzzled Japanese tourist.

Waz, the Frank "Lefty" Rosenthal of our group, has become very adept at this game. He can tell you if the whore is high on crack or smack, often both in some cases. He can also tell how many pints of lager are swilling around in the punter or if they are stoned or high on cocaine.

A strange-looking man walks by with a small tree growing from a pot on his head, bringing a whole new meaning to the word *pothead*.

I rush out and take his photo, and he gives me a lump of cheap Moroccan hash as some kind of insane reward. He reminds me of someone I know back in Scunthorpe, but I can't think who.

As more pints of lager are ordered, the search for enlightenment continues. So we score some quality marching powder from an old friend and the night gets into top gear. As things start getting messy, we lose some of the group and end up in Excalibur another cool pub with its legendary heavy-metal jukebox. Now, I must admit I enjoy a good line of Amsterdam's finest yayo just like the next man, but I hate sniffing around in dirty toilets like some kind of drug fiend, so I convert euro into porn and visit a private polishing booth just around the corner. A two-minute walk, two euros in the slot, two barrels of bugle up the hooter, and bingo! I rise sniffing to the vision of a naked munchkin wrestling a farmyard animal.

"Oh my God!"

Frantically, I hit the forward button and now a dwarf has hold of a cat by its tail!

"What the fuck!"

I unbolt the door and race out quickly, and for a moment I feel total weightlessness, then pain and shock as I clatter heavily onto the floor with the wind knocked out of me and my head smacking hard on the glossy tiles.

I can't breathe, let alone speak, as the big mop man helps me to my feet in front of an audience of United Colors of Benetton faces.

I limp out clutching my ribs and rubbing my head as my Good Samaritan gets to work mopping up the gentlemen's spendings.

"Too little too late, you useless fucker!" I shout back while limping my way painfully back to thebar.

"Are you OK, Eddie? Shall we administer first aid?" Waz laughs.

"Yeah, get me a double Jameson's! I just went fucking flying in that porn booth place," I wheeze in agony.

"He slipped in *spunk*." Waz laughs, telling everybody in the pub.

"It wasn't *my* fucking *spunk*!" I protest vigorously.

"Haw, haw-haw-haw-haw," they all laugh.

"Glossy tiles," I retort.

"Haw. Haw. Haw."

I can't laugh; it's too painful.

"Anyone fancy taking some magic mushrooms?" asks Waz, thankfully changing the subject.

**\* \* \* \***

The next morning I've got a lump the size of an ostrich egg on the back of my head as an array of hallucinogenic flashbacks pollutes my mind, and I'm sure I've broken at least two ribs!

As well as this, a Columbian flu epidemic has hit our group, and I sneeze painfully, wondering why I keep doing this kind of shit to myself. I can't wait to get on the Camino and chill out and hopefully sort my life out. Waz keeps bringing up the spunk skating incident every ten minutes, but I don't care. I'll be the one laughing when I get to Spain with naked Euro chicks dancing round a big fire on the beach. "You just wait and see, Waz!" I tell him.

I say my goodbyes to the group and walk up to the train station in pain. My ribs twinge as my heavy pack compresses each vertebra in my already-weakened body.

"Five hundred miles! Bloody hell, I can hardly walk five hundred meters!"

On the train all alone, anxiety grips my fevered mind as Amsterdam disappears from view. The trolley man comes past, and I buy four Heinekens for the trip (all fifteen minutes of it).

Outside the airport foyer, I smoke my last joint to calm my frayed nerves before my flight. On the third pull of my smoldering Bob Marley, my weakened brain implodes into six million broken pieces and my life crumbles around my feet as alarm bells ring out in my panic-stricken paranoid brain!

"*Miiiinnnndddd ffffuuuucccck*!"

In a flash I throw the joint in the bin, then the twenty grams of hash I had stashed in my sock and the bag of philosopher's stones in my boot. "What the fuck was I thinking?"

I frantically check my pockets and wallet for any more contraband.

"Hang on, I smell burning! What the fuck ? Shit, the joint!"

Smoke puthers from the bin as I delve in like a drunken hobo, rummaging through smoldering newspapers, carelessly discarded drugs, and chocolate wrappers. Finally I locate and extinguish the rogue spliff with a can of Heineken. Then I quickly dash inside the building before I cause a bomb scare and end up in hand and leg cuffs, wearing an orange romper suit with a sack on my head on the next plane to Guantánamo Bay, no doubt.

I check in and aim straight for the busy airport bar, hiding underneath the peak of my hat while nursing a pint of lager as a deep, dark depression sets in.

The first pint calms my nerves and I psychoanalyze my actions of the last few months leading up to this point.

The second and third pints deal with the intense feelings of fear and self-loathing, and the fourth and final pint of lager steadies my nerves for the plane journey.

I sweep up the pieces of my broken life and head for the terminal.

# BASQUE COUNTRY

I'M HOLED UP IN A CHEAP HOTEL and spending like a drunken sailor on shore leave, with nothing to show for it except a very bad hangover yet again. This week I've been mostly drinking sherry, wine, port, and brandy in an array of Spanish, Irish, and Australian bars and even a midgets' disco. I thought at first it could have been a children's disco, but then I noticed that nearly everyone seemed to have a mustache and were all drinking beer and wine, so who knows? I finally bit the bullet and bought a guidebook about the Camino, with photographs, maps, and historical facts. Thirty euro it cost me. It's more expensive than the Bible, for Christ's sake! And I don't even feel like reading it yet, with its pilgrim this and pilgrim that, No, I still don't like the sound of it one bit anyway.

Today's the day of Lindsey's wedding, and I know I'm

missing out on a fantastic party. I wish I was back there now helping her celebrate the big day while eyeing up the talent at the reception, plus funky dancing in the disco later on and getting ripped, royally pissed, with all my good friends in a luxury stately home environment. But here I am in a dingy hotel bar all alone reading about Andy McNab in Iraq.

Could be worse I suppose?

Early next morning the rain is coming down at all angles as I march through the storm toward the bus station. I feel like SAS trooper Eddie McNab on a mission, my pack heavy with thousands of rounds of ammunition, hand grenades, and ration packs with an M16 rifle and grenade launcher ready to defeat Saddam. Mind you, on the news it said that Saddam had gone AWOL, missing in action. MIA.

I bet he'll show up in England at some point claiming asylum and hundreds of thousands of pounds a year in handouts plus a four-bed semi in North London like that other one-eyed scrounging, hate-filled, hook-handed twat off the telly.

As I trip over a paving slab, I'm brought back to reality when the heavy pack jolts my spine. The tight, torturous straps cut deeply into unaccustomed tender flesh as a cold, wet wind blows through collar and cuff and my ribs are absolutely killing me.

McNab says always follow the rules of the seven Ps:

Proper, Preparation, and Planning Prevents Piss-Poor Performance.

It feels like I've followed the last three! I honestly thought Spain would be boiling hot like on the holiday television programs, but I'm getting soaked to the bone in a force-ten gale, and I curse myself yet again as a wintry gust blows me into the bus station.

The pungent aromas of nicotine, piss, and diesel fill the damp air.

I notice a group of dodgy-looking winos gathered in a corner out of the cold, drinking from an array of mysterious bottles and tins. Their needy-pleady eyes meet mine as I pass by, reminding me to check my pockets for my passport and wallet.

Now all I need is a bus ticket and a platform number and I'm all set, so I prepare by learning a few useful words on my Franklin W7 Euro translator.

Eng: *Ticket.*

Esp: *Billete.*

I reckon before long I'll have this language mastered. It seems you just add an "el" in front of a word or a vowel at the end of another word and you're almost there! A lot of the words are the same as English, so I'll have it sussed in no time! Armed with guidebook, phrase book, and Franklin, I approach the ticket booth ready for action.

*"Hola. Buenos días, señor. Uno billete para Saint-Jean-Pied-de-Port, por favor. Muchos gracias,"* I say politely.

For a brief moment I thought I'd solved the mystery of missing Saddam, but on closer inspection I can't ever remember him being four foot tall. Nevertheless, little Saddam scratches his head and goes into spasm, bouncing around on his stool like an excited child while barking and panting like a small dog. All of a sudden he starts pointing outside at the rain, and, to make it worse, I find myself mimicking his actions as people behind me in the queue start sighing and barking too.

Little Saddam stops to breath for a split second, then

resumes his high-pitched yakking and yapping while yet again pointing outside at the rain as if it somehow holds the key to my salvation. I can't take any more.

Back out in the downpour I search for clues like Scooby-Doo. I even try asking some of the Spanish travelers, but they all shrug and bark at me too. In my guidebook, it says that Roncesvalles is pronounced Rons Cheese Valleys, so that's settled, it should be easy?

Then one particular sentence gives me a fantastic idea.

"Spanish teenagers are amongst the best educated in Europe and most of them speak good English."

"That's it! That's all I need to know!" So I scan the bus station for likely candidates. Unfortunately there are not many to choose from, but here goes. . . . She might look like a cross between opera singer Pavarotti and a small yeti, but she is nonetheless a Spanish teenager and hopefully well educated.

"*Hola, Rons Cheese Valleys, por favour, señorita,*" I say, smiling with my eyebrows raised in gleeful expectation. The girl begins to giggle demonically and in slow motion her head does a full 360 degree turn, thankfully followed by her body.

"Mmm," she giggles again as foam and dribble appear at the corners of her mouth, her face bearing an uncanny resemblance to a heavy-metal-loving pirate I once knew. She takes the guidebook and studies it intently for well over a minute. I can almost hear the gears in motion inside her brain. Her mouth opens. . . .

Here comes the answer, here comes the answer. Anytime now . . .

"Cheeeeee," she lisps through her clenched metal teeth,

covering my page with spit and foam.

"Cheeeeee." She giggles again, fluttering her eyelids and juggling her mono brow, then finishing her performance with a ballet twirl and a blank stare.

I'm still none the wiser, but now she's holding the book and doesn't seem to want to let go. I pull, she pulls, we both pull. But as I try wrestling it from her, she digs her fingers in even harder. She's surprisingly strong.

Luckily, a stern-looking gentleman hurries over to us, balling and barking as the girl loosens her grip and starts to cry.

As he drags her off across the station floor, she keeps looking back at me like it's somehow all my fault. She's then thrown in with a group of even odder-looking children, all looking back at me strangely.

One of them has a special helmet, while another ticks violently, shouting at an unseen force. I watch as they all scuttle off holding hands, all still staring at me, followed up by a matronly lady wearing an apron.

I can't believe it.

My next attempt at ticket purchase descends quickly into a strange game of charades against an old lady with one tooth. This time I find myself pretending to drive a bus and saying Ron Cheese Valleys a lot. As I go through the gears she barks and grunts while I struggle to suppress the urge to fling my guidebook across the concourse like a Frisbee and shout "fucking hell" at the top of my voice as Basque Jeremy Beadle appears dressed as a bus conductor and the whole place erupts into laughter.

The rain is somehow the clue. I cool off outside again but still find nothing. So in my notepad I draw a stickman with rucksack, a large bus, and a mountain and have written the name "RONCESVALLES" in great big letters. Now even a child would understand it, not that I'm going to ask one mind you, although . . . let's not rule that one out just yet!

Third time lucky, I approach cautiously. This time the booth is manned or should I say womaned by a ferocious-looking person with jet-black hair and bloodred lips, with her eyebrows missing from the normal place but now drawn on with thick black marker pen farther up her forehead, giving her both a look of surprise and outrage. The last time I saw a face this scary it was tattooed on the back of a Japanese yakuza gangster I made friends with while staying in one of Her Majesty's detention houses in Perth, Australia, 1994.

The water demon growls as I approach. I fearfully show her my guidebook and hand her the drawing.

*"Hoy,"* she barks!

*"Hoy,"* I bark back, not knowing what the hell she's on about.

She holds up two fingers, a V for victory maybe? Finally things are looking up as she stamps one of the tickets and slides it under the counter, still barking while I bow out backward like a royal subject. "Yes, I did it!"

So, with the ticket firmly in my grasp, it's now time to get to my next challenge—to find "the platform."

After half an hour of more charades, pointing, barking, clapping and almost having a fist fight with a drunken tramp, a small nun kindly tells me that the only bus goes from platform six at six o'clock. Now it's eleven thirty in the morning—well, at least I haven't missed it.

I'm in two minds whether or not to go back into town and hit the theme bars for a few hours, but I take one look at the downpour and I'm straight back in the station bar with McNab, coffee con leche, and cigarettes, keeping a keen eye on platform six for any kind of action, hoping to spot my first pilgrim.

* * * *

At close to 5:00 p.m., platform six comes to life with the arrival of a gang of rowdy Gore-Tex-clad gray-haired pensioners, then a ZZ Top look-alike with a fat druid covered in seashells. Next on the scene is a small cowboy wearing a poncho and Wellingtons, followed by a fat red-faced German man in a safari outfit. Then a medieval wizard arrives in a thick brown cloak. But where are the pilgrims in the stovepipe hats and buckledy shoes?

Maybe I've got it all wrong as usual? The whole scene looks like some kind of bizarre Hieronymus Bosch nightmare on LSD.

Anxiety hits me again. The nun must be wrong. I'm at the wrong platform! Where are all the hippie girls and the cool dudes with guitars? Where are all the Suzies, Siobhans, Sarahs, and Maries?

In a panic I enquire at the front of the queue just to finally make sure I'm in the right place.

*"¿Roncesvalles, por favor?"* I ask the hatchet-faced crone.

She turns to me with cold dark eyes, devoid of emotion, and then brays at me like a mule while pointing harshly to the back of the queue.

"I should definitely have gone to Ibiza." I sigh to myself as I drag my heavy pack through the diesel and cigarette butts, wishing I was on a beach now with a cold beer, watching the girls go by instead of this utter madness.

I watch with grim expectation as a jolly young man approaches and politely asks the same crone with a great big smile, *"¿Roncesvalles?"*

The drunks in the corner look up from their booze as another mule-like bray echoes around the station. Now the not-so-jolly young man has a big frown on his face, probably thinking the same thing as me.

At the back of the queue he wipes the rain from his glasses and we exchange looks of bewilderment, eyeing each other suspiciously.

"Excuse me, are you going to Roncesvalles by any chance?" he asks in a clipped Oxbridge accent, but our introductions are cut short as the bus pulls up and all hell breaks loose!

All of a sudden the excited fat German and ZZ Top begin to squabble like children, and in the fracas ZZ stamps hard on the foot of an old Dutch lady, who kicks him in the shins, tugs his beard, and shoves him back into the fat German, who throws a wobbler, almost blinding two small ladies with the dangerous trekking poles on his pack!

Brazilian voices start up like chainsaws as the druid and the cowboy seize the moment and charge for the door like a pair of human wind chimes—closely followed by fat safari suit, ZZ Top, and the Dutch lady, all with packs on and all trying to squeeze onto the bus at the same time.

"Manners maketh man!" I shout down the queue.

"Quite frightening, aren't they?" says the posh fellow.

"I've seen better behaved football hooligans, Cigarette?" I ask him.

"No thanks," he says, sighing. "I only smoke Silk Cut. . . . Rob," he adds, extending a cold, wet flannel of a hand.

"Eddie. Nice to meet you," I say. "Bloody foreigners! Eh."

We're last on board and there are still plenty of places to sit. I don't know what all the fuss was about!

The bus pulls out into the pouring rain, and I wipe the condensation from the window to stare out onto the pleasant green land.

"I thought the rain in Spain fell mainly on the plain," I say gloomily to my new friend.

"Looks more like wet Wales to me," says Rob cheerily.

I look across at him and he looks strangely familiar, reminding me a lot of Jarvis Cocker from the Sheffield-based indie band Pulp or Charles Hawtrey from the *Carry On* films crossed with a poorly equipped member of Enid Blyton's Famous Five series.

Whatever the weather, he certainly looks a proper bobby dazzler in his national health glasses, with the obligatory piece of sticking plaster holding them together. A 1950s backpack by his side, with an old-fashioned watch on his wrist, and thick woolly socks and Jesus sandals on his feet! I wonder for a moment if he's just been left all this shit in a will. On his paper-thin cagoule, an array of badges and pins catches my eye. One of them is the famous *Blue Peter* badge, but it's upside down—no doubt some anarchistic studenty thing. I make a mental note never to ask him about it, as I'm sure the reply will be a long, drawn-out tale of double-sided sticky tape and used toilet rolls, all without parental permission.

Cocker, as I now decide to call him, tells me his plans.

Firstly, he's going to walk the Camino for ten days. Then he'll take a bus to Madrid to meet his parents for a small break, after which he hopes to rejoin the Camino farther down the road, and time permitting, will be in Santiago de Compostela before the month's out.

"That's the plan anyway," he says with a shrug and a shake.

I shiver too, feeling a dramatic change in temperature as the bus climbs higher into the cloudy mountains. As the light quickly fades, we eventually pull up in the darkness.

"Well, this must be it," I say, rubbing my hands excitedly together, but just what I'm excited about I'm not quite sure. It certainly isn't the company or the weather, that's a fact!

I double-check with the driver that we are, in fact, in Roncesvalles and not Ron-says-bollocks, and we step off the bus into the eye of the hurricane.

As the bus pulls away, ZZ Top, the wizard, fat safari, and the entire rabble suddenly vanish off the face of the earth as we stand in the pouring rain getting wetter by the second. First we run toward a streetlight and an old stone building with the word "Hotel" on the side.

I squint across the expanse of potholed tarmac, seeing in the distance the illuminated sign "Bar," so all's not lost. I hand my guidebook to Cocker and light a cigarette. He may as well be of some use.

The monastery stands before us, silhouetted against an angry black sky looking more like something of a horror film and not the Spain I had imagined at all. We're still getting wetter and wetter, and any ideas of catching a bus or taxi from here to Saint-Jean-Pied-de-Port have been blown straight out of the water.

I'm tempted just to head straight to the bar, but the bad weather has us running for cover into a large stone barn, where most of the people from the bus queue, including fat safari, ZZ Top, and the wizard have joined other Bosch-faced erberts to form a new, unruly gathering around the only exit and entry point to the building. I can't believe it.

So we turn on our heels and run back out, into the rain

across no-man's-land to Dracula's castle as a flash of lightning illuminates the night sky and a crack of thunder rattles my bones and brain.

"Some weather we're having," I say to a wretched soul.

"Huh, rain," he laughs, looking at the sky as his squinting face gets a flurry of hailstone.

As we run through the tempest, my ribs are totally killing me and Cocker plays leapfrog with the deep puddles in a futile attempt to keep his feet dry. In the porch he wipes his glasses, reminding me a bit of Velma from *Scooby-Doo* when she loses her glasses,

"Maybe there's a better place to sleep here in the monastery?" I ask.

"It doesn't say anything about it here," he says, staring into the book.

We follow the herd into a large room, and the odor of sanctity hits us as opposed to the odor of insanity back at the barn.

Thankfully, it looks like we've come to the right place. On the big oak table before us are the fabled Pilgrim's Passports, the credentials that will enable us to enter all the hostels or pilgrim shelters along the way. At the end of the table sits a stern-looking priest with half-moon glasses perched on a long nose with immaculate Brylcreem hair.

He checks, stamps, and views all passports with an unnerving glare. His presence alone has put the anchors on any ill behavior from the pepper-pot hooligan posse.

I fill in my name, address, passport number, and next of kin.

"Next of kin?" I say. "It's not exactly base camp Himalayas, is it?"

*On foot, on horse, on bicycle?* is the next question.

"On foot," I write. That was easy.

*Reason for pilgrimage?*

Now this is a tricky one, considering my misfortune of late: Get fit, walking holiday perhaps? I fought the law and I lost?

"Hey, what are you putting for that one?" I nudge Cocker.

"Mmm, I don't know," he says, spying on the next person.

"Spiritual," he secretly whispers before handing his new passport to the wise old priest. The priest looks puzzled, then looks back at Cocker, then at his passport, and then down at his sandals.

"A pie?" says the puzzled priest.

"A pie," says an equally puzzled Cocker.

The priest shrugs and stamps his passport, wishing him well, his transformation from pillock to pilgrim now finally complete, and now it's my turn.

"Mmm." He looks me up and down and then at my new credentials.

"Irlanda, Catholic, hmmm?"

"Yes." I nod with a cherubic smile as he looks straight into my soul.

The priest looks puzzled yet again.

"What means this? Reason for pilgrimage . . . for the . . . how do you say this . . . craic? What is craic?" He frowns with piercing eyes.

Suddenly I feel myself shrinking like Alice in Wonderland and wish I'd have just wrote *spiritual* like everyone else.

Think, man!

"It's Irish for God," I squeak from the floor.

"Ah, spiritual," he says, happily stamping my new passport and ticking the box.

*"Buen camino,"* he says, handing it back.

"And a *buen camino* to you too, Father," I say, feeling immediately idiotic, as it's highly unlikely that the Holy Father will be donning his Berghaus in the morning.

Cocker and guidebook have now established that the only place to sleep around here is in "that barn," which is free, or in the hotel for thirty euros, thus translating from pocket to brain that there is thirty euros' worth of drinking tokens available for tonight.

"Happy days; let's dump these packs in the barn and lift the latch, as they say!"

"Sounds like a plan," says Cocker, with his glasses fogged up again.

Ghoulish faces huddle by the doorway of the ancient building, making entry impossible yet again.

"Excuse me, please. Sorry. Can we get through?" I ask politely.

Nobody moves a muscle.

*"Hola, s'il vous plaît,* sorry, pardon, *excusez-moi!"*

"They must be deaf as well as stupid!" I say loudly to Cocker as we squeeze through, much to their annoyance.

The whole place smells like a big wet sheepdog with bunk beds as far as the eye can see. Saggy pensioners in saggy underpants with saggy faces all shuffling around aimlessly while a topless granny has a flannel wash and an old man clips his toenails. So we make for some beds in the farthest corner of the barn far away as possible from this lunacy epidemic.

"MASS 8:00 P.M." I laugh at the large imposing signs on the walls, not that that makes any difference to us, as we shall be in the "BAR AT 8:00 P.M."

Cocker agrees. Beside our new beds we prepare for the evening and Cocker strips down to his boxer shorts, revealing pierced nipples and a Celtic dragon tattoo all down his arm! Could be a dark horse, this lad? There's certainly more to him than meets the eye, that's for sure.

"I reckon I should have gone to Ibiza instead," I say to my new friend as a loud grating voice punctures my left eardrum.

*"Jam njam, yakyakkay, mmnnignggg, babadabadabdab . . . yakyahyakyakyakyak."*

"What the fuck? Who the fuck's this now . . . ?"

The Japanese tattoo face from the bus station has come back to get me! But now in an apron with different eyebrows, like some kind of ogress or something! How can this be? Cocker stands frozen with his trousers down in a state of shock. Whatever this disgruntled nursery rhyme character is barking on about, she is far from happy, that's for sure.

She snaps an order at Cocker as he shuffles around with his trousers still to his ankles, and we hand over our new passports for inspection. She studies them like a Gestapo officer for what seems like an eternity and then examines us with her beady eyes before sharply handing them back as we stand before her giggling nervously like naughty schoolboys.

*"Yak yak yak, mak, nak, kak."*

Her high-pitched yakking starts to pull on my nerves like fingernails down a blackboard.

"English please! ¡No comprendo! ¡No understando!" I protest.

*"No. No. No, yak, yak, yak,"* she says, pointing to the numbers on the beds and waving two pieces of paper from out of her apron: 63 and 65.

We are in beds 8 and 10. "What's the big deal?" I ask her as she hands us the mandatory paper numbers and points harshly up the room while grunting at the sign on the wall. MASS 8:00 P.M.!

*Yeah right,* I'm thinking to myself.

We quickly leave the scene of the crime, with Cocker trying to pull up his jeans, pack his stuff, and walk at the same time as her shrill voice starts up again. We're halfway up the room when she stops for breath and turns her attention to the old man clipping his toenails.

He shrinks away in fear as her high-octave yakking cleanly removes a small piece of his sanity like a jackhammer on a steel plate.

I quickly locate my most important piece of equipment, my orange earplugs, and show them to Cocker.

"I hope you've got some of these, mate. There's going to be some serious snoring tonight, I reckon!"

"I don't need them," he says. "I can sleep anywhere."

He then begins a tedious tale about when he and his friends, Edgar and Justin, were at some pop festival and him waking up in the mosh pit as the Prodigy exit the stage. "That's how well I can sleep," he adds.

I'm not really listening; I just want some beer.

I arrange my kit on the bed; luckily I got the bottom bunk of the mechano bed, with Cocker on the top of another set of bunks.

I dread to think about our new bunk buddies, but to be fair, I'm past caring now. I'm just wondering what the hell I've got myself into.

An excitable silver-haired man makes his way around the barn, talking to everybody he meets. He's also the first person I've seen actually smile today. His energy is infectious as he works the pensioner druids and wizards up into a frenzy. Could this be the infamous Pablo Coolio? I wonder.

"Are you going to the Pilgrims' Mass?" he's asking everyone.

"Good, good, yes, yes, yes," he says, pleased.

"Ah, you are going to the Pilgrims' Mass?" he asks as we attempt to flee.

"No! We're off to the bar for a—"

"Nooooo!" he shrieks, and the barn falls deathly quiet.

"No," I say, feeling like Oliver Twist.

"Nooooo! You are *not* going to the Pilgrims' Mass?" he shrieks.

Suddenly a pang of good-old Catholic guilt renders me speechless in the silent barn. The ogress looks up from her apron and grunts, pointing at yet another Mass sign on the wall.

"I guess we're going now," sighs Cocker.

We squeeze back out into the storm and run for our lives to Castle Vlad again, closely followed by the excitable man and an array of different-sized and shaped pilgrims, while most of the others are happy to stand around the door and stare at the rain.

The church is dimly lit and we file in quietly, well almost. It's been a long time since I was in a Catholic church—I'm always the one standing when I should be kneeling, kneeling when I should be standing, and talking when I should be listening. The priests file in and we sit down, then stand up, then kneel down. As per usual no one has a clue what we're supposed to be doing, and a Mexican wave of uncertainty flows through the pews twice.

At last the Mass begins, first in Latin, then in Spanish, then in French by different priests, and I'm getting very bored and my legs and ribs are aching like mad with all this sitting and standing malarkey. Eventually, the German priest finishes and an Irish priest steps forward and conducts the final Mass in English, asking the Lord to give us strength for our long days ahead on the Camino de Santiago, and finally, at last, it's over.

"Thank the Lord," I say.

I feel happy; everyone is smiling, shaking hands, and hugging each other. Cocker and the excited man seem to be having a competition of hugging the most people in the least amount of time and space, often hugging the same person thrice in the frenzy. Something compels me to leave the melee and follow the others up to the altar.

For the first time in my life I take the flesh and blood of Christ, as I feel I may need every bit of help I can get on this journey, starting now. So, with the ceremony complete and the rain a disguise for our desperation, we, newly ordained pilgrims, run to the bar across the flooded tarmac like the charge of the Light Brigade.

I'm quite surprised and somewhat miffed that the bar is full of people, none of whom were at the Mass. I quickly order three pints and scan the bar for pretty girls as Cocker and Mr. Excitement shout at me through to the restaurant to join them in the first sitting of dinner.

"First come, first served!" shouts Mr. Excitement.

"Free wine!" shouts Cocker.

I'm in there like a shot as the tables fill quickly with windswept and wet post-Mass pilgrims. We fill our glasses with red wine and toast to our future success. Our new companion is called Jean Nicolai. He is a fifty-five-year-old Swiss man but lives in Brisbane, Australia, with his young wife and works as a physiotherapist. A cheeky glint appears in his eye. "I also organize rave parties out in the bush," he says.

Wow, there's certainly more to this guy than meets the eye, that's a fact. Never judge a book by its cover! Twice now in the space of an hour; first Cocker, now him—well it takes all sorts I guess.

Cocker proudly announces that he works for Islington Borough Council as a cultural officer and graduated from Cambridge last year.

I can almost see him punting up and down the river in his blazer like a complete Gaylord, wearing a straw hat or answering stupid questions on "University Challenge" with the rest of those erberts. I'm pleased to leave all the talking to them, really; there's no point telling them my recent stories of woe.

Our first course begins with soup and concrete bread as Cocker tries in vain to catch the attention of the busy waiter without actually bringing attention to himself, the way a lot of posh people do. The English way of not wanting to cause a scene. The busy waiter sees his foolish bibbling but chooses to ignore him.

"When I've finished the Camino," says Jean Nicolai, "I'm going to Ibiza to meet my wife, dance like crazy, and take ecstasy!"

Cocker splutters, almost having a seizure!

"Ecstasy?" we both say.

"Oh yes, yes, yes, and why not? I like it. Don't you?" he says. "I'm a DJ too. Do you like dark psytrance?" he adds.

Cocker is stunned. "Aren't you a bit old for that?"

"No, no, no, not at all. Don't you like dancing? I love it." He laughs, doing a little rave shuffle in his chair. If I didn't know any better, I'd say he'd had some ecstasy a couple of hours ago and was buzzing his tits off with his yes, yes this and no, no that all the time, talking at a hundred miles an hour about how he met his wife and where they live and that she's only thirty-three and he is fifty-five!

"Well, you're only as old as the woman you feel," I tell him, and we high-five. I immediately like the guy; he's happy and full of fun, unlike most of the others his age. I wonder if he's brought any X or MDMA powder with him. I'll ask him later, 'cause there are plenty of people around here who could use some, by the looks on their faces. Me included.

"You can't beat a good-old disco biscuit, can you?" I say.

"Definitely not," says Jean Nicolai.

"But they don't make them like they used to!" I tell them.

"You never tried X then?" I ask Cocker.

"Oh you should." Jean Nicolai nods. "You must!"

"No, I smoked cannabis once, though," he says.

The second course consists of a whole trout, with its glazed eye staring coldly from the bright-green plate, along with a small handful of thinly cut chips. The colour suddenly drains from Cocker's face, looking like he could be sick any minute. He brims his wineglass, has a big gulp, and tries in vain yet again to attract the attention of the busy waiter.

"Are you all right?" says Jean Nicolai.

"You look a bit green," I tell him.

"Doesn't he? He looks green!" shrieks Jean Nicolai, quite delighted.

"I don't eat fish," sighs Cocker, picking at his chips.

As the meal draws to a close, I liberate a bottle of wine from an empty table before the next sitting of wet pilgrims arrives. We hear more of Jean Nicolai's tales of superstar DJ'ing in the desert and the joys of MDMA powder. I've decided to call our new friend "Swiss John." It's easier that way.

I can't be doing with difficult fancy double-barreled names.

A group of Dutch teenagers swamp the bar with their volumes at full blast. All seem to be smoking big trumpets of shag tobacco, yet only quaffing light refreshments, thus requiring question to their ages and their being here. Thankfully, they drink up and leave noisily.

"Ah, peace at last!" I stretch and grimace as my rib pops.

"Three more San Miguels," I say to Cocker. "Get the beers in!"

"No. No. No!" shrieks Swiss John, pointing at the clock.

"Whoa, keep your hair on, man; it's not last orders yet!"

"No. No. No. It's nearly ten o'clock, the curfew!"

"The curfew? What *are* you on about?"

"The curfew. They lock the doors at ten o'clock!" he shrieks.

"What?"

Sure enough, the bar is empty and the horrible truth dawns. . . . It's two minutes to ten, so we rush out into the storm once again.

"I can't believe we never sung that pilgrims' hymn in the church: 'He who would valiant be, 'gainst all disaster, let him in dee dee dee . . . follow thy master . . . la dad a dah dah dah . . . and care not what men say . . . '" I sing.

"'We labor night and day to be a pilgrim,'" sings Cocker, finishing up.

"Yes, ya bastard." He knows the song.

I punch him lightly on the shoulder and throw my arm around him as we sing out loudly, splashing forward into a pothole.

"To be a pilgr—fucking hell!" he screams, much to my amusement.

Cocker has finally sworn. It didn't take long but that's what you get for wearing sandals in the rain and drinking on an empty stomach.

But then again, I can bring out the worst in some people.

The ogress stands guarding the door, rattling a bunch of keys and ranting like a demonic jailer.

"Hi, gorgeous, bed number 33, here he is," I joke, pointing at Cocker, who looks like a drowned rat. The ogress growls and points at his sandals, words firing from her mouth like an antiaircraft gun, and if looks could kill, Cocker would be hung, drawn, and quartered.

More people have arrived now, and the place is filled to the brim with half-naked pilgrims. No half-naked Suzies, Siobhans, or Clares in their Ann Summers lingerie—just Ethel, Mavis, and Nora in their floppy pants and bras.

"No wanking tonight," I joke as I climb into my loudly creaking toy bed. Cocker takes his glasses off and immediately falls asleep.

Lucky bastard! I'm still wide awake. I begin to think back to my younger days in the backpacker hostels of Australia and some of the crazy things we used to get up to. Our favorite pastime at one point was to go into the dormitories when everyone was asleep and shave off our fellow backpackers' eyebrows for "the craic," as we called it. Thirty-three people we did in one night after a massive party.

One unfortunate girl woke up minus her eyebrows and half of her 70s muff. Really, we should have received medals, but the hostel owners and most of the browless didn't share our enthusiasm and we all got kicked out!

My friend Phil Charles came off the worst; he woke up to

find he had been tattooed from head to toe in black permanent marker with a great big black cock on his forehead *and* his eyebrows missing, but most alarmingly the mystery artist (Steve Powell) spent extra time completely coloring in his cock and balls—and what made it worse was poor-old Phil got chucked out too, guilt by association!

I must give Powelly a ring at some point!

I look across at sleeping beauty and wonder, but my mischievous ideas are cut short by the arrival of our new bedmates. I shut my eyes and try to remain calm as the bed shakes, rattles, and rolls with its new occupant.

As the foreign tongues of naked pensioners vibrate around my tired brain, the lights suddenly go out to a loud chorus of screams and shouts from all four corners of the room, followed by a long comedy trumpet fart, a young person's laughter, and loud snoring.

I spot the ogress lurking in the shadows, waiting and watching, on patrol.

The bed sways backward and forward like a sailor's hammock. Whenever I move a muscle, I wake the old man above and vice versa. In the middle of the night the whole bed shudders and shakes as the old man has a coughing fit, and once again I'm wide awake and desperately need a slash. Fearful of the ogress, I venture into the cold cavernous underground toilets, expecting her to jump out and bollock me at any minute. As the snoring reaches epidemic levels, I return to find both my earplugs missing.

# DAY OF DAYS

*"I laugh when I hear that the fish in the water are thirsty. I laugh when I hear that men go on pilgrimage to find God"*

—KABIR (1440-1518)

THE UNDERGROUND TOILETS AND SHOWERS are full to bursting, as is my bladder. I walk in and immediately walk back out again as the sight and sound of a naked German with a big stupid face and a tiny acorn for a cock, who happily engages the shuffling masses in morning conversation. I meet Cocker on the stairs looking like a misplaced holidaymaker, with his wash bag and towel slung casually over his arm.

"Watch out for the sausage smuggler," I warn him.

"What?" he says all bleary-eyed.

"Don't drop your soap!" I say, warning him seriously.

It's six o'clock in the morning and pilgrims including fat safari, the wizard, and a strange wailing/shrieking woman gather by the door, surveying the rain. As I walk past, cross-legged back to my bed trying not to wet my pants a gust of wet wind blows in and chills me to the bone.

Luckily our two bedmates are nowhere to be seen, and I manage to clean my teeth in peace. I sit on the edge of the bed and rapid exhaustion finally sets in; I could sleep for an eternity as I spot the ogress sweeping the floor and yakking like a madwoman.

I find my missing earplugs under the bed covered in gray pubic hairs and grit as Cocker comes back from the bathroom shaking his head.

"Why is there a naked German man down there?" he asks.

"Fuck knows! Pilgrims' Hospital, they call this!"

"It's more like A FUCKING MENTAL HOSPITAL!" I curse. "Look at it."

Cocker looks around the room and then at the crowd gathered by the door.

"Doesn't look like anybody's going anywhere this morning." He sighs.

"Fuck that," I say. "I need to be on. I can't stay here a moment longer or I'll go completely mad!"

Cocker thinks for a brief moment, jumps down off the bed, and quickly begins to pack.

"Right, I'm ready!" he says, pulling on his pack and smiling.

"You're ready? Are you kidding me?"

"No, why?" he says, looking down at his green woolly socks

and sandals. "I prefer to wear these. I've had them three years. They've done the Pennine Way, the Inca Trail, Croagh Patrick, and Ayers Rock, I'll have you know!"

"Where are your walking boots?"

I'm in no mood to stand and debate his idiotic situation.

He's wearing them, not me.

"Come on, let's go!"

I stick a cigarette in my mouth, light it, tighten my straps, and I'm ready for action. Cocker looks like a cross between a boy scout and a train spotter.

"As the shepherd said to the sheep dog: Let's get the flock out of here!"

Our exit is blocked, but not for long!

"Coming through, get out of the way, move, move, and move!"

I need to piss like ten horses, so I shove my way out like Moses parting the Red Sea, only this time it's a Red Sea of raincoats with gray clouds on top closely followed by Cocker in his Egyptian sandals.

"Hey, hey, watch out!" they moan in their mother tongues.

"No smoking in here," shouts fat safari.

We stand for a moment in the monsoon, trying to get our bearings.

"Well, this is it; this is what we came here for. Adios, dickheads!"

We wave goodbye to the shocked faces at the door.

"To be a pilgrim!" I shout, raising my fist in defiance at the lightweights.

"Follow zee yellow brick road," shouts a squeaky Italian woman.

"Stick to zee road," shouts one of the druids.

"The yellow brick road! What yellow brick road?"

"No, the yellow arrows!" shouts Cocker through the wind.

"The yellow arrows? What yellow arrows?"

"The yellow arrows that lead us to Santiago," he says, pointing at a splodge of yellow paint on a tree.

Luckily for Cocker it's a puddle-free track, with no one in front and no one behind. We're wet through in minutes, but I'm glad of his company, so I hand him one of my trekking poles to use as compensation. I knew it was a stupid idea to bring them.

"Did you have a hat yesterday?" I ask him.

"No, why?" he shouts, looking like some kind of demented pixie, with the pointed hood of his cagoule pinning his ears forward so he can hear what I'm saying through the gale.

"You look different somehow," I tell him.

After half an hour or so we reach the village of Burguete and find a nice quiet café bar with us its only customers.

"Peace at last," I sigh.

We order our coffee and cake, shivering like junkies at a funeral.

My back is soaked with sweat, and I can feel the straps of my heavy pack cutting deeply into my shoulders like some kind of medieval torture device. Cocker blows into his hot coffee and panics, checking his pockets, then the table, then the floor, searching and longing but for what? The hot coffee solves the mystery, as it hasn't steamed up the lenses of his glasses because they are still back where he left them beside the crowded sink at the asylum. And just like Velma from *Scooby-Doo*, Cocker needs his glasses! Mystery solved?

"Fuck, fuck, fuck, fuck," he swears all the way back to Roncesvalles as I contemplate life over another coffee and make use of the pristine, fragrant, and uncrowded bathroom facilities.

A few equally bedraggled pilgrims arrive, and after half an hour, so does my wet companion, having added another six kilometers to his journey.

The café starts filling with grumpy wet pilgrims, including the big fat, stupid, loudmouth German acorn-excuse-for-a-cock naturist.

He's now happily telling everyone at the top of his booming idiotic voice that there are "No!" places to stay in between here and a place called Larrasoaña. I fear I may have to kill him painfully if we ever meet again!

* * * *

We leave the café and plod on through the streets of Burguete, with the rain steadily getting worse and the puddles getting bigger and deeper, and with the paths more treacherous and downright dirty.

As we cross a small bridge onto a muddy trail, I feel a horrible chill from the toxic sweat on my back. So I try snuggling into my pack for warmth, pulling the sleeves over my freezing fingers as I shiver, shake, and slide through the wet mud. My bones tremble and lungs pound with every slippery step, each cell in my body crying for mercy.

My companion has gone very quiet now, using all his energy to leap to and from sparse bits of dry ground while trying unsuccessfully to avoid the deep puddles and then across the Basque countryside come the immortal words.

"FUCKING HEEELLL! MY FEET ARE BASTARD FREEZING!" he screams.

I stifle a huge laugh as my Gore-Tex boots splash through another puddle as he stands there, up to his knees in a great big muddy hole. Then we walk along in cold silence, and eventually he resigns himself to his fate, splashing angrily through the puddles like a naughty boy on a crap school outing.

*Why am I doing this again?* I ask myself. Oh yes, I remember: I'm doing it for the criac! Why did I write that, even? It's not true; in fact this is quite the opposite of craic . It isn't craic at all. I'm sweating from the inside out and soaking wet from the outside in.

My pack gets heavier and heavier, soaking up more rain, with the straps biting deeper and deeper into soft flesh. We stop in the relative shelter of a wooded glen. I need my waterproof trousers, and where are they? Yes, there, at the bottom of my pack! I dig them out as Cocker shivers and shakes, and to save time I try to pull them on over the tops of my muddy boots. "FOOL!" As I raise one leg into the pants, the other slips and I find myself on my back *again*—this time in mud, luckily.

Cocker is now almost hypothermic and realizes the error of his ways. Should he die today, his express wish is for his memorial to be inscribed, "Unprepared for Everything."

I assure him I will attend to any funeral arrangements just so long as I get to keep his sandals. It's agreed. Our bodies dampen, but our spirits lighten as we laugh in the face of adversity and trudge onward despite our ever-growing problems.

Now, not to be outdone by his lack of rain cover, Cocker stops and asks me to pull the back of his cagoule up and over the back of his pack in a vain attempt to stop the contents getting wet. This only adds insult to injury by exposing his bare chest to the elements, robbing Peter to pay Paul, as they say, and giving himself pneumonia at this rate.

Up ahead a solitary woman makes slow progress in the mud.

*"Hola,"* she says cheerily, trying to place one foot in front of the other.

*"Hola. ¡Buen camino!"* I say to the second person I've seen smile in two days. She's Brazilian, so it's time to resort to universal sign language.

"Rain." I point to the sky.

"Cold, yes?" She laughs and shudders.

"Santiago?" I point ahead.

"Ha, yes." We all laugh.

She's a happy old soul, but up in the distance is her not-so-happy companion, leaning against a tree.

*"Hola. ¡Buen camino!* Cheer up, only another 499 miles to go," I joke.

Her face says it all.

**\* \* \* \***

On the steep inclines my legs are pumping like a steam engine and I'm beginning to overheat. I can't get my breath, my lungs are fit to explode, my legs are swelling, and my body is reaching meltdown.

The trousers that are cutting off circulation to my whole body did once belong to me, only they got too tight, so I kindly gave them to my cousin, and like the fool that I am, I borrowed them back off him to go on this walk. So here I am today in this completely idiotic situation, and to make matters worse, seconds later I'm flat on my back in the mud again like an upturned tortoise with a small stream of dirty water running down my sleeve and another down the crack of my arse.

"Pull them off me, man!" I plead, waving my legs in the air.

Cocker yanks hard at my trousers, pulling me along through the mire as he manages to free one leg. Then with a huge effort he frees the other, and a wet streak of mud splatters his face and the inside of his glasses.

*Splat!*

My laughter echoes through the valley, and when I stand I award him the filthy Gore-Tex trousers as some kind of Camino compensation. Then he washes the mud and grit out of his eye with contact lens solution.

"At least it's not spunk," I tell him.

"What!" he shrieks.

"Spunk! I slipped in spunk in Amsterdam and broke my rib."

Cocker blinks in disbelief.

"Don't worry, it wasn't my spunk," I tell him.

* * * *

High in the mountains we eventually begin our descent down a very uneven trail that the rain has turned into a fast-flowing stream. The going is treacherous and rough, with Cocker trying to stay out of the icy water as I, on the other hand, am just trying to get to the bottom in one piece. As I jump down onto a large boulder, my knee cap almost pops out of its socket, and I feel a sickening pain as muscle tears.

"Hang on!" shouts Cocker, coming to the rescue.

As he helps me to stand, I suddenly feel icy cold and my

teeth start chattering in shock. Painfully we get to a tarmac road, but at the other side there's even more danger. This time I find myself crawling and kneeling in icy water, but I slip again, and now something rips in my back as the muscles twist and spasm, locking me up solid in immense pain.

"Wait here," says Cocker. "I'll go for help."

"From where exactly?" I ask him.

He thinks for a moment, realizing we're miles from anywhere, and this time he shakily accepts my offer of a cigarette. As we smoke like doomed men before the firing squad, I realize that there's nothing I can do except to carry on regardless until I drop.

Thankfully, no more waterfalls cross our path, only farms with horrible, ferocious barking dogs on taught chains that I pray are well tethered.

Eventually we pass through a valley and a wooded glen with a beautiful green river running beside us. We come to rest at an old bridge close to some dwellings and smoke again to rejoice in our stay of execution, as we've made it to Larrasoaña at last, safe but not sound!

We follow the yellow arrows into the village and pass a small gray-haired old woman taking very slow, tentative steps, almost on tiptoes. She is obviously in immense critical pain.

*"Hola. ¡Buen camino!"* we shout cheerily.

Our salutations go down like a lead balloon. She just answers with her stone-cold glare. Just leave me to die! I want to laugh at the irony of the situation, as the woman who, although soaked to the bone and at death's door, has bothered with a special plastic cover for her hat!

"Are you all right?" asks Cocker in a soft voice.

She is too tired to even speak so we leave her to die and crack on as Cocker keeps looking back anxiously while I limp along in agony, scanning the streets for any kind of welcoming sanctuary or medical facility.

In the distance I see familiar pilgrim-type faces loitering around a doorway with intent to cause me misery.

# SANDALS AND SEX OFFENDERS

IN THE COLD WINDSWEPT FOYER of the pilgrims' hostel, the old woman floats in like a ghost and collapses in a heap. I try to help but I can't move; my body is locked, frozen solid. Thankfully, Cocker leaps up to her aid and a couple of kindly ladies rush out of a dormitory and spirit her away, never to be seen again.

Maybe I ought to try that trick? I could do with the same treatment myself.

A tall, immaculately dressed Dutch man saunters through and smugly announces with a joyous grin that the dying old lady has taken the last bed.

It takes awhile to sink in. "What! Hang on a fucking minute. How can she have taken the last bed?"

He nods, shrugs, and sits down in front of us, mocking us

with his presence and his ironed shorts.

Soon more poor, bedraggled souls turn up, and yet again the smirking man tells them with a huge smile that there are no more beds left. With a self-satisfied look, he pulls out a book and begins to read as the atmosphere turns to one of utter hopelessness.

Insanity rules in my fragile state of mind, and I find myself on the very edge of despair.

Suddenly from out of nowhere, a small aggressive man appears, barking and shouting. He picks one of my boots up by the lace and shouts at the muddy floor, and then at the rest of our dejected group.

The Dutch man looks up from his book, shaking his head and smirking at our misfortune yet again, and disabled or not, if he does it one more time, I'm gonna crawl over there and bite his kneecaps off!

As the little man whizzes around the room like a demented spinning top, my damaged brain translates his barking into English, telling us yet again that there are no more beds, shouting in our faces like white noise inside my head, driving me totally and utterly Billy Bonkers.

I need to get out of here quick!

"Cocker, help me!"

"Cocker."

Suddenly, he jolts out of his trance and slowly helps me to stand.

I take a very long, deep breath and hobble barefoot out into the cold rain to smoke my last cigarette as my mind wanders over the hills and far, far away.

"Come on. Eddie, there are beds upstairs," says Cocker,

tugging at my sleeves.

"What?"

As if by magic, the barking devil has now suddenly transformed into an enchanting little angel. Showing us the toilets and the showers, where we can hang our wet clothes, then finally he shows us our icy little room with five mattresses on the floor, like sardines in a tin.

"Jesus, it seems colder in here than it is outside!" says Cocker.

I'm third in line for a cold shower, where I inspect my wounds and try to straighten my twisted train wreck of a body. Then it's back to the subarctic bedroom, where I change into wet joggers and wet T-shirt, and crawl into my wet sleeping bag on my soon-to-be-cold, wet mattress.

At least we've a room to ourselves. I couldn't be sharing such a confined space with a load of these so-called pilgrims. Physical pain I can cope with, but mental pain, that's another story altogether.

Another three mattresses lie next to us and I begin to worry.

Cocker comes back from the bathroom wearing a brand-new pair of gleaming-white Dunlop sex-offender training shoes. I force a painful cackle at his terrible choice of footwear again, and then I cry, "Fuck me! I knew I had forgotten something. Extra fucking shoes!"

Cocker's face breaks into an enormous grin as a group of rude and noisy French pilgrims arrive, shattering the peace, and a big red face pokes around the door, rudely demanding beds.

"All taken," says Cocker, saving our sanity a little while longer as we prepare for our trip into town.

* * * *

First, I'd like to be rushed to the accident and emergency department of the local hospital, followed by the chiropractors, clothes store, knee specialist, and last but not least, a shoe shop. We only make it as far as the local bar and decide upon a little drink for medicinal purposes to warm our cockles and thaw our souls, setting a new world record for drinking a bottle of red wine in seventeen seconds flat. As the waitress comes back with our change, she's off again to fetch another bottle.

"May as well fetch two!" I shout, but she doesn't understand.

"Ah, the Blood of the Pilgrim," comes the mysterious voice and we look up from our raised glasses at the strange, small olive-skinned man standing before us.

"The wine. The Blood of the Pilgrim, we call it," he says proudly. "You have walked from Roncesvalles today?" he asks.

We nod as he sits down and introduces himself as Manuel from Madrid. Considering he came the same way, Manuel is miraculously clean and dry. He takes a small device from his pocket and announces that today he's walked 23,098 steps.

"I have lost five stones in weight," he says, delighted with himself.

"Jesus, by tomorrow there will be nothing left of you." I laugh, but he doesn't understand the joke and turns down our invitation of a glass of wine. Swiss John arrives with a very sexy companion he has met en route. *Hola.* she smiles and takes off her padded jacket to reveal a stunning cleavage, and Cocker's glasses steam up as if on cue and yet another joke falls on deaf ears.

I prepare to order some food from the pilgrims' menu.

The waitress comes over and I pick the same for myself and

for Prince Charming here. He is now too busy chatting to the Spanish girl's lovely boobs; and all interest in food has gone. Manuel sternly waves his finger, warning us both not to drink any more wine. So, in response to his idiotic suggestion, we refill our glasses and order another bottle as he stares at us bug-eyed.

"Where are you from?" Cocker asks the girl.

"Salamanca," she replies in a lovely Spanish lilt.

"I'm Rob and this is Eddie," he says, and we shake her soft little hand.

"Hi, I'm Belen," she says with a pretty smile.

"Bell-end? No way!" I protest as Cocker frowns angrily.

"No. It's Belen," she says. "Like Helen but with a *B*."

The innkeeper arrives with soup and bread, and we tuck in gladly, but Cocker starts playing with his food like an irritating child, separating his peas from his ham and clanking his spoon on the side of the bowl all the time. When the innkeeper comes back to collect the plates, he points down at the pile of ham on the side of Cocker's plate.

*"Buen jamón. ¿Qué pasa?"* he says, shaking his head, rubbing his mustache. *"Jamón buen jamón,"* he keeps saying, outraged as the room falls silent. Belen begins to translate.

"Why haven't you eaten your bacon?" she asks Cocker.

"I'm vegetarian," he says like a big dandy.

*"Vegetariano,"* she tells the innkeeper.

*"Vegetariano,"* the innkeeper snorts, rolling his eyes. *"Vegetariano,"* he shouts, pointing at Cocker, and the whole place erupts into laughter.

"What's wrong with that?" he moans.

"It's not a great part of the country to be a *vegetariano*," she tells him.

We all laugh this time, and I laugh the loudest, because the innkeeper brings me two legs of chicken with chips and Cocker only chips.

"I can see this being the start of a great partnership," I laugh.

We toast with full glasses, and Manuel toasts us back with his step counter. He laughs for a moment and then frowns as I pour more wine. We even get an unexpected dessert, which Cocker eats with gusto.

Swiss John seems very quiet today, though. I get the impression that the wind has been blown out of his sails, as he's a shadow of his former self—or maybe the ecstasy has worn off?

So, well wined and dined, we hobble back up the road and get collared by the barking man at the front of the hostel, waving at us to come inside. It soon becomes apparent that this man, in addition to running the pilgrims' hostel and barking a lot, is also the major of this town and will stamp our pilgrims' passports.

He gestures us into his office with exited little yaps and seems to have taken quite a fancy to Cocker's gleaming white trainers. As he shows them off to the barking major, we also reestablish that Cocker is indeed doing the Camino de Santiago on a pie, and now the pair of them appear to be doing a drunken cancan.

"I'm doing it on a pie," he keeps saying, flicking his legs in the air.

"Would that be a chicken and mushroom or *vegetariano?*" I joke.

Cocker thinks it's hilarious and wacky like some kind of silly, Pythonesque sketch, but even a thick bastard like me can conclude the other two answers were on horse or on bicycle. "A pie" means doing it on foot and not a salad dodger's food item.

It doesn't take a degree in social science to work that one out, I can tell you.

Back in our cold, claustrophobic room we have two new roommates: a jovial Frenchman called Pierre who's busy bandaging some serious foot wounds, and an American guy in expensive walking gear who calls himself Tucker. There's one mattress left, and Tucker says the body of a pilgrim has been found back on the trail.

A chill goes up my twisted spine.

Back in my damp sleeping bag I count my blessings and eventually drift off into a disturbed slumber . . . with . . . strange . . . dreams.

An intense light shines out from an alien spacecraft hovering above, blinding me into a state of confusion. I'm frozen solid, unable to move as the strange, inscrutable beings standing above me merge into familiar faces I recognize. I see the smug Dutch man, the ranting ogress, the Japanese tattoo demon, fat safari and the acorn-cock German, all babbling incoherently. Suddenly bolts of thunder and lightning shake the room as the devil major leaps out of a black cloud in a red spandex rock music suit with goat's horns on his head, cackling like a witch.

I scream in agony as he stabs me viciously in my knee and ribs with a three-pronged trekking pole while barking orders to his crazed disciples. The smirking Dutch man grabs my arm and the loudmouth German grabs a leg, as do the ogress and the water demon, with the little devil leading the way out through the crowded hostel, barking and shouting while the other pilgrims chant like zombies to the English punk band The Stranglers' hit song "No more heroes."

"No more pilgrim anymore! No more pilgrim anymore!"

At the entrance, the major gives the order, and I'm cast out into the freezing rain, naked and with no shoes.

I wake abruptly in a world of pain, soaked in horrible freezing sweat.

The thought of failure and going back to Scunthorpe is too much to take. I can't give up on the first day, for fuck's sakes. In a moment of clarity I find the answer and get to work on my heavy pack.

The small tent can go, the camping stove and cooking pots too, the wet toilet roll, wet pair of jeans, and three of the wet T-shirts, the fold-up chair (also wet), the self-inflating roll mat (wet), three of the paperback books (also wet), and last but not least, the Frisbee

Cocker wakes from an equally disturbed sleep and we quickly decide that the best course of action we could take from here is to go down to the bar, get exceedingly pissed, and see how we feel in the morning. So it's back on with the torture boots and into the rain we go.

* * * *

The innkeeper and his family are sitting around a table enjoying their evening meal. He shakes his head and snorts loudly with a mouthful of *jamon* as he spots Cocker. "*¡Vegetariano! ¡Vegetariano!*" they all laugh, chewing on bones and fish heads.

We huddle by the blazing fire, drinking like there's no tomorrow, not speaking but sighing a lot. So as darkness falls on another day in Larrasoaña, we drink up and wobble back up the road. As we reach the hostel, Cocker stumbles and falls flat on his face in the wet gravel in front of an array of disgusted pilgrims. Luckily I'm carrying the wine. Cocker flaps around on the ground like a drunken haddock and then eventually picks himself up and bows to his aghast audience like a circus performer. With no round of applause, we disappear out of harm's way to the indoor/outdoor kitchen facility.

Tonight at Casa Eduardo:

We dine from the legendary British army ration pack, awarded five Michelin skid marks by army master chef Paul Bástard.

For a starter I have the meatballs and Cocker has the boiled sweets, bourbon biscuits, and cream crackers.

For the main course I have chicken curry, and due to his *vegetariano* requirements, Cocker has rice with curry sauce, and because of my kind nature, he can have the whole chocolate pudding all to himself.

"I'll sleep well tonight," I say, rubbing my bloated stomach as he eats the pudding, studying the wrapper.

"Bleugh." He coughs, spitting it all back into the bowl. "Fucking hell, I thought it tasted funny. 'Consume within five years, or before 1996,'" he reads. "We've been poisoned!" He shrieks with panic in his eyes.

"Don't be silly!" I laugh, drinking the rest of the wine as my stomach inflates worryingly.

"These are OK, though," says Cocker with another mouthful of boiled sweeties.

On the way back to the room we spy Swiss John laid out on a mattress, laughing and joking with the gorgeous Belen, with her sweet little face smiling away, tucked up all warm and snug in a lovely red sleeping bag. Cocker interrupts them by announcing that we've just poisoned ourselves with out-of-date army rations.

2:17 a.m.: I wake up with a painful jolt, not knowing which is worse, the alien that is about to burst out of my bloated stomach or the screwdriver twisting in my back, knees, and ribs!

The alien kicks painfully from within as I double up in agony, rushing down the corridor like a wounded soldier, hoping and praying that the toilet is empty. Once inside I remain cold and motionless for the next two hours, staring out the glassless window at the ancient countryside, peaceful and serene except for the high-decibel snoring coming from every room, sounding like tanks rolling up the street.

Back in the damp room I feel totally shattered, and yet again I've lost an earplug. I search in the darkness but to no avail as French Pierre snores next to me like a donkey with the flu. I kick him some more and he stops as I try to doze off in the small window of opportunity. After several attempts my lights finally go out, and the light in the room comes on.

I look at my watch—it's 5:30 a.m.

# MOMENTS OF DOUBT AND PAIN

FOREIGN VOICES FLY up and down the corridors like evil spirits, and I clearly hear Swiss John saying something not very good about the weather—words that I don't want to hear. My body feels shattered, bloated, and full of poisons as I lie there freezing, imprisoned in my toxic tomb with what feels like a screwdriver jammed in my back and a chainsaw tearing at my knee.

I desperately need a slash, but the bathroom is occupied, and yet again I wash my face with the wet corner of my towel and brush my teeth, swallowing the contents.

Cocker opens his eyes. "Fucking hell" are his first words as he emerges from his death knoll. He stands, scratches his head, then his balls, and slopes out to the bathroom with his wash kit, and ten seconds later he's back in the room trying not to piss himself.

I open the window for a peek at the weather and a cold wet wind blows back in, bringing with it a feeling of total despair, then more despair and distress as I squeeze back into my wet, cold boots.

We slowly make our way out through the busy hostel to the al fresco kitchen for the last of the out-of-date coffee and hot chocolate, which we end up mixing together.

Cocker is complaining of a hangover, but mine has yet to surface as my other problems have taken precedence. We both water the grass and Cocker projectile vomits with his willy still in his hand, much to the distress of the morning misérables.

On the way out of town we pass the inn, and a group of gloomy-looking pilgrims, including the fat acorn-excuse-for-a-cock German are huddling around the entrance trying to keep dry.

As the storm steps up a gear, Cocker wants to stop and join them.

"Sanity before pain! We need to keep moving," I tell him.

We cross a bridge and continue downhill along a tree-lined path next to the river. He eventually stops moaning and comes alive, telling me about his trekking adventures in Borneo, the Great Wall of China, Nepal, and the Himalayas—then Croagh Patrick in Ireland, Ayers Rock, and part of the Pennine Way.

"All in these sandals. I've had them over three years," he says proudly.

"Yes, but they are not waterproof, are they?" I remind him as his woolly, wet feet slosh along. "I reckon you're gonna get trench foot."

"No, I won't, they dry out quickly," he says.

"Yes, but they get wet quickly too, you erbert!"

Eventually he stops babbling about his beloved sandals as

the going becomes treacherous yet again. In a heavily wooded area we completely lose sight of the arrows and follow a dark forest track to a total and utter dead end. As we turn back, the wind blows my poncho backward over my head, twisting it around my neck, strangling and suffocating me at the same time. I try in vain to free myself before ripping it off in a fit of rage and watch angrily as the wind whistles it out of my wet hands high into the pines. Despairingly, we trudge back the way we came, coming at last to a tarmac road. In the distance we see a pilgrim smoking a cigarette, and as we get closer the guy looks a lot like Benny Anderson from ABBA, decked out in a spotless raincoat, khaki trousers with an ironed crease down the middle, and white trainers. His accent is Italian and he kindly directs us back on track with a big happy smile. Soon we're picking up the arrows again and getting covered in more and more mud as I start to wonder about Benny and his aura of cleanliness. I look back, but he's vanished.

"How come that guy was so clean?" I ask.

"Maybe he came a different way," says Cocker.

"What different way? We've mostly followed those yellow arrows since the off, apart from when they disappear, so if he came the same way as us then it's a bloody miracle!"

"Maybe he was some kind of angel sent to guide us," says Cocker.

"What, looking like Benny from ABBA? Don't be stupid." I laugh. "I met an angel once," I tell him.

"Yeah, a Hells Angel, I bet!" he yells.

"No, a real angel, from God!"

"Where?" He laughs.

"Jerusalem, 1991," I tell him, and begin my story.

In the lounge of an old hostel in the Arab quarter I noticed a strange-looking man staring into space. His appearance intrigued me, as it was the middle of summer and he sat there in sweltering heat wearing a red mohair jumper with thick leather biker trousers, and beside him was a battered guitar. I thought it rather strange and lit up a smoke.

"May I have a cigarette?" asked the stranger in a foreign accent.

I threw him the pack and watched him carefully take one out, study it for a moment, and light it, almost setting fire to his curly blond locks.

"Sank you," he said, sounding like Arnold Schwarzenegger.

I watched as he smoked like a child, coughing and spluttering, and holding the cigarette like a pen.

"Where are you from?" I asked him, noticing a German accent.

"Heaven," he said. "I'm an angel from God!"

"What, like Gabriel?" I laughed.

"Yes," he replied innocently.

"Are you on medication?" I asked him.

"No!"

"Should you be?"

"No," he replied, shaking his head.

"OK. So how long have you been an angel from God exactly?"

"Four thousand years, more or less," he replied as quick as a flash.

"OK. What did you do before you were an angel then?"

"I lived in Atlantis."

"You lived in Atlantis. Can you swim?"

"Yes, and I can fly," he said.

"So, when's Jesus coming back then?"

"He's already here," said the angel.

"Where?"

"Our Lord is everywhere!" he said, looking all around.

"So, how did you end up here in Israel then?"

"I flew," he said.

"El Al? Tel Aviv?" I asked him.

"No. I flew here on my invisible golden wings," he said, unfazed.

On that note, I was actually inclined to believe him! Because how the fuck had he gotten through the Israeli border control with answers like that?

"What's your name?" I asked him, expecting something comically biblical.

"Terry," he said.

"Terry?"

"Yes, my name is Terry," he said.

I couldn't believe it. Terry, the angel? Maybe he was an angel or maybe he was full of shit. But there he was living, breathing, and talking utter bollocks, so take your pick. By day two everybody in the hostel was bored with his constant lunacy, so angel Terry went back to staring into space and bumming cigarettes from unwary backpackers. No one saw him eat anything, drink anything, go anywhere, or wear anything different, and on the third day he announced that he was leaving for Africa and would anybody like to buy his guitar?

I wouldn't have minded it for myself because according to the angel Terry, the guitar could play itself.

\* \* \* \*

Back on the road the grand citadel of Pamplona comes into view and it's happy days walking along the tarmac path beside the banks of the river. I feel better than James Brown, but Cocker is lagging behind like a total gaylord, moaning about his feet and totally getting on my nerves. I've got ten times more injuries than him, and if he'd chosen proper footwear for this journey, he wouldn't be in such a state.

"Stop a minute, please, stop. I've got a stone in my sandal," he cries like a baby. I want to slap his face and shake him. I feel embarrassed for him and embarrassed that I'm with him, and as we go over a bridge with an ancient cross, he puts his head in his arms, sobbing tearfully while removing another sharp stone from his idiotic footwear. As we set off again, he starts whining that I'm walking too fast for him.

"You and those stupid fucking sandals! Pull yourself together for Christ's sake, man, we're almost there—warm showers, wine, and women," I tell him.

But two minutes later he's at it again, with tears rolling down his face as he sobs into the wall of the citadel in yet another hissy fit.

"HI, BELEN! How's it going?" I shout out in bedevilment.

Cocker leaps to attention, looking in all directions for the pretty girl and wiping his gaylord tears from his glasses and face.

"You. Total. Bastard!" he moans as a couple of red-faced ladies pass by.

"Well, imagine if she saw you acting all silly like this," I reason.

As we set off, he huffs and puffs, but my form of persuasion has done the trick, give or take a few angry reminders. On the steep hill into the city the yellow arrows finally give way to golden scallop shells illuminating our path to salvation.

We eventually find the hostel opposite a shoe shop, and I'm seventh and Cocker's eighth in line. So we kill time by eating some very old, very sticky boiled sweets, and a stern-looking graybeard tells us to watch out, as there are thieves around! So with Cocker on guard, I take the opportunity, at last, to buy a pair of sandals.

On my return a small lady with a large key arrives and all hell breaks loose as we push and shove our way up the creaky spiral staircase into the old building with our pilgrims' credentials at the ready.

This time I'm top bunk in another Meccano bed and Cocker has a bottom bunk on a different bed. The place quickly descends into bedlam as more and more people arrive, with every available space filled with drying clothes and drying bodies all getting in each other's way.

My stress level is on the rise as I wait my turn for the showers, and as one of the rude Frenchmen exits, I dive in quickly, coming face-to-face with his heavily-skid-marked undercrackers hung from a peg at eye level. Luckily, a French hand comes around the door and whisks them away before more psychological damage can be done to my raging mind. I angrily bolt the door and step knee deep into a stone-cold shower tray, with pubic hair and Band-Aids blocking the plug hole.

I curse like mad, twiddling the taps until one comes off in my hand and a jet of icy water hits me in the chest like a water cannon.

\* \* \* \*

The time is 1:30 p.m., and we're still in one piece, so we celebrate another success with pilgrims' blood in the bar opposite the hostel.

"Well, we made it again," I say, shaking Cocker's wet flannel of a hand, and he takes one of my cigarettes, saying yet again that he normally only smokes Silk Cut.

"I doubt they even sell Silk Cut in this region." I laugh, pointing to the cigarette machine.

"Why's that then?" he says, spluttering.

"*Vegetariano* type of cigarette," I tell him.

We drink and smoke our way to the bottom of the bottle, and the rain finally stops as we get our first glimpse of Spanish sunshine.

"Hurrah," beams my posh pal, rolling up his jeans and exposing his translucent legs.

"Whoa! Put them away, man. You'll get us arrested," I joke, but the sight of his knobbly knees is sending me over the edge. So I tell him I'm going to find the internet café and we make promises to meet later for an evening meal.

I'm feeling a little iron deficient, so I head straight to the Irish pub for a few pints of the black stuff, because what's good enough for racehorses and pregnant women is good enough for me too!

In the bar I order my pint and sit quietly reading my pilgrims' guide as a sexy little waitress brings me a very fine-looking pint of Guinness and a plate of free tapas.

I quite like the writings of these medieval pilgrims. One of them, in particular, has an edge I can associate with.

The French pilgrim Aymeric Picaud says of the Basques:

They are a barbarous people unlike all other peoples in customs and characters, full of malice, swarthy in colour, ill favoured of face, misshapen, perverse, perfidious, empty of faith and corrupt, libidinous, drunken, experienced in all violence, ferocious and wild, dishonest and reprobate. Impious and harsh, cruel and contentious. Unversed in anything good, well trained in all the vices and iniquities, like the Geats and the Saracens in Malice and everything inimical to our French people.

In certain regions of their country, that is Biscay and Alva, when the Navarrese are warming themselves, a man will show a woman and a woman a man their private parts.

I seem to remember my father saying something along the lines of this on his first-ever visit to Scunthorpe, but he got straight to the point by saying to my mother, "I've never seen so many miserable bastards in my whole life."

The Navarrese even practise unchaste fornication with animals. For the Navarrese it is even said that they hang a padlock behind his mule or mare so no one can come near her but himself. He even offers libidinous kisses to the vulva of woman and mule. That is why the Navarrese are to be rebuked by all well informed people.

Aymeric also says, "Their language is like the 'barking of dogs,' and they force strangers to take down their trousers."

"They force strangers to take down their trousers? Wow! That would be great," I say to myself, looking across at the sweet, smiling waitress. She reminds me a bit of a girl from the

Basque region that I met in a bar in Clonmel, County Tipperary, back in Ireland.

She was as pretty as a picture until she opened her mouth. Her face twisted into a sneering mask of hatred, hating everything and everybody, saying she wanted to join the IRA so she could learn terror tactics to blow up politicians back in her own country. Nice girl, really, but definitely in need of some hardcore anger management of the sexual kind.

A young man wanders in and starts his shift behind the bar, busying himself in chatting up the two waitresses. He sees me waiting but chooses to ignore me. Eventually, he comes over.

"Yep?" he sighs miserably.

"Pint of Guinness, please."

"Yep," he says again, looking down his nose at me like I'm a piece of shit on his shoe. "Three euro fifty," he sighs again in an Australian accent, holding out his hand and moaning because I haven't got the right money.

"Oh, and some more tapas while you're at it, mate." I nod.

He slinks off, muttering under his breath, then returns minutes later, throwing the plate down next to my drink. Then he's back to laughing and joking with the girls as I start to imagine how his head might look in a slowly tightening vice.

Returning back to the guide, I can't believe what I'm reading. It says there are two routes from Roncesvalles to Larrasoaña, and instead of choosing the good earth track or the tarmac road, Cocker and I chose the "Very stony, steeply rising paths. Then the very uneven path with loose stones, and the very dangerous descent from Erro Hill, with loose stones and many torrent courses."

And today, instead of choosing "the tree-lined path and

asphalt road," we chose "the hillside path, a very dangerous one and not to be recommended."

Fantastic! Follow the yellow arrows, said Cocker, and it's no wonder that angel Benny from ABBA and Manuel were so clean.

"Stick to the road!" shouted the German at Roncesvalles. "Bloody hell!"

Again the little wanker is ignoring my empty glass on purpose, the fucking little prick, obviously fresh out of Australia and at the pre-violent-assault stage of his young life.

He saunters slowly over, smiling at girls and then looking all serious at me. "YEP?" he goes again.

"You wouldn't happen to know where the internet café is, would you, mate?" I ask him politely.

"What do you think I am, mate? Tourist info?"

It takes me a while to count out my change as he moodily stands, sighing before me.

"You wouldn't be going to England at all, would you?" I ask him.

"Why, what's it got to do with you?" he says, all tense.

"Just wondering; that's all."

He wanders over to the till, glancing back at me with a worried look on his face as I fantasize about giving him a vicious right hook to his ribs, so he can remember me on every breath for the next three weeks. It's crazy to think that a puny little midget like him would be so rude to someone twice his size. I deduce, therefore, that he has never been properly assaulted yet. I know I don't have to do a thing, because in three months' time, Brenda and Bill Douglas of Claremont, Perth, Western Australia, will be getting a call from the emergency room somewhere in south London to determine the blood group of their son so they can safely remove the broken glass from out of his cheeky little face.

I return to my book and check if there are any easier routes to Puente la Reina. Thankfully, there's just one path.

I've had enough of reading about churches, old battles, and what medieval pilgrims had to say. With what this is costing me, I could have gone to Thailand, never mind Ibiza! This walk has just been a nightmare from the start. At least I met Cocker, who's provided me with a little light relief, but it has to get better than this, surely.

But the fearful question hits me: What am I going to do when the pilgrimage is over? So I consider my options:

Go to San Francisco to work with Powelly? ☺    ☺

Go back to Holland? ☺    ☺

Go back to Scunthorpe? ☹    ☹    ☹    ☹

That last thought alone plunges me into despair and anger.

"Hey, mate," I call as he slowly makes his way over with a face on. "Another pint," I say, handing him my glass.

"Yep."

As he goes to grab it, it slips from my fingers and smashes onto the tiled floor.

"G'DAY, MATE!" I hobble out of the now-silent bar.

Back at the hostel, Cocker looks up from his book.

"Where on *earth* have you been?" he shrieks. "I've been looking for you all over the place."

"I went for a pint of Guinness. I was feeling iron deficient."

"Iron deficient? Have you eaten yet?" he whines.

"No."

"Well, we should get something to eat. We've got a long day tomorrow," he says, going all serious all of a sudden.

"I'm going for a siesta. Give me a shout in an hour or so," I tell him.

I climb onto my bunk and stare at the ceiling, immediately wishing I'd brought a personal CD player or something. Instead, I listen to people's Euro babble, and now I find I've climbed up here, I need to take a leak, so I jump down painfully.

"Rickety bastarding bed! Aaaagh!" My leg almost buckles.

"Where are you going now?" Cocker shouts.

"I'm going for a piss! Is that OK with you?" I shout back, as shocked gray stares follow me out the door "I don't believe it." Every single cubicle is in use, even the women's toilets. I can't wait a second more, so I run across the street, dive straight into the bar, use the gents', and order a large beer. Sorted.

Half an hour later the quest for enlightenment has brought me back to the Australian theme bar and the company of some rather plump but foxy Canadian backpackers called Sheena and Lisa. The girls are traveling around Europe on a year off. They are a great craic and certainly know how to drink, so we buy endless rounds of whiskey and Baileys on the rocks, and at last I'm having a good time.

The last thing I remember is ordering three double Jameson whiskeys.

I dream I'm in a hotel room with the two Canadian girls romping naked on the double bed, beckoning me over with their eyes while doing exceedingly rude things to each other.

"Here comes Eddie!"

I leap in between as they smother me with their huge, soft breasts, and . . .

*Ting, ting, ting, ting, ting.*

"What the fuck is that?"

The girls shrug and then disappear from view as the stark interior of a Spanish jail cell comes into focus.

A gruff-looking cop is standing there smoking, while banging a saucepan with a small hammer.

I can taste the whiskey on my breath as he gives me back my belongings, including five crumpled postcards of the running of the bulls.

"*Buen camino, peregrino*—no more whiskey." He laughs hoarsely.

I bum a cigarette off him and find my way back to the hostel. It's 5:30 a.m. again. It feels like Groundhog Day.

I just want to get out of this town, never to return again.

I spot the pepper pot posse'and ZZ Top gathered by the door, and yet again I need to piss like ten horses and yet again all the toilets are occupied!

"Jesus Christ! What do these people do in there?" I ask myself.

I find Cocker packing his stuff, with a big red mark on his left cheek. He's totally outraged.

"Where on earth have you been?" he protests angrily. "You smell like a paraffin lamp," he says, screwing up his face.

"Is that posh cockney rhyming slang for smelling like a tramp?" I ask him.

"No, you do actually smell like a paraffin lamp."

"What's happened to your face?" I ask him.

"Oh, it's nothing. I tripped into a bedpost in the middle of the night going to the toilet," he says, rubbing the mark.

And so for the third day running, I clean my teeth sitting on the bed and wash my face with the wet corner of my towel. Then, during a fit of rage, I rip the zipper out of my sleeping bag while standing cross-legged trying not to piss myself yet again.

# MUD AND LAUGHTER

AS WE CROSS THE PARK I finally seize the moment to empty my bladder. "*Hola, buenos días.*" I wave to one particular woman looking over in horror at me. She turns away in disgust to watch her fat Rottweiler curl one off next to the children's swings.

I think I'm still drunk. What on earth happened to me last night?

I remember being locked out of the hostel and being in the Irish bar again. But after that I dunno. I dread to think. It's in the past as far as I'm concerned. Speaking of which, in the distance is the remarkable contrast of past and present, with Cocker in his great-granddad's walking gear representing pilgrims from the 1870s to 1970s era and Tucker representing the modern-day pilgrim in his pricey North Face and Berghaus. I catch up with them and find Tucker is busy taking the piss out of Cocker's sandals. For an American he has quite a wicked sense of humor, but then again I bet even the Aborigines and Tibetan monks were pissing themselves laughing when they saw Cocker coming down the road.

"So, where did you end up last night then?" asks Cocker.

"If you must know, I met a couple of sexy Canadian girls in the Australian bar, and—"

Tucker interrupts. "Whoa. Canadian girls, dude. They sure know how to party," he says approvingly, giving me a loud high five.

"Why didn't you come and get me?" Cocker whines.

"I did come back for you, man, but the hostel was locked up. I was knocking for ages!"

"So, where did you sleep then?" he asks.

"The Hotel Europa," I lie. "The girls said I could sleep on their couch in their room, so . . ."

"And?" says Cocker, looking well and truly miffed.

"What do you mean and? Surely you don't need me to explain what happened next, do you?" I laugh.

"Yeehar!" Tucker punches the air. "Hey, well done, man, you got laid! Awesome news, dude!"

"Yeah, but I think I might have snapped my banjo string, though. It was like riding a bucking bronco. No, wait a minute, two bucking broncos." I laugh, rubbing my bellend for Cocker's benefit.

"Yeeeehar!" wails Tucker again in my right earhole.

"I'll get you to rub some cream on it for me later, Cocker."

"I will not," he says. "I hope you used a condom with those girls."

"I used quite a few," I tell him.

"Yeeeehar!" wails Tucker in my left earhole with another round of high fives as Cocker shakes his head.

"This is a religious pilgrimage," he says, "not a trip to Benidorm!"

"Hey, at least you never got bitch-slapped by an old lady," says Tucker.

"What . . . ? That was an accident; it's his fault!" says Cocker, pointing at me.

"Why is it my fault? I wasn't even there," I respond.

"He bitch-whipped and then he got bitch-slapped, dude," says Tucker, laughing.

"I didn't mean to hit her like that; it was his towel," he says, pointing at me yet again.

"Oh, so it's not my fault then. It's my towel's fault. You whipped an old lady with my towel, and it's the towel's fault. You really are a bad mofo, Cocker," I tell him.

"It cracked like a bullwhip, dude, and then she got up and bitch-slapped his face." Tucker laughs.

* * * *

It's a busy day on the Camino, with lots of new faces and more younger people, thankfully, including the ever-so-noisy Dutch students and a tall Brazilian guy with a huge Afro and a guitar strapped to his back, casting a strange silhouette in the distance.

I chat with a friendly Austrian man and a nice Danish girl, who have both just started this morning, as have many others.

In fact, it seems like a lot of people have started in Pamplona.

Why didn't I just start here, and who says you have to start in Ronsaysbollocks, anyhow?

In the foothills of the Sierra del Perdón, the past rains and constant procession of pilgrims has turned the path into an out-and-out quagmire. My boots soon become three times their size, covered in heavy clay, and all unnecessary conversation has died.

A backpack lies abandoned in the mud—possibly someone suffered a mental or physical breakdown right here. Probably both.

I grit my teeth and crack on, stopping every few meters to literally kick the mud from my boots, sending lightning bolts of pain from knee to rib to back to brain to mouth, and to top it off my hangover is kicking in badly. I find Tucker sitting by the side of the trail, cutting the clay from his boots with a dangerous-looking knife. So we rest for a while on our packs, laughing at the hapless Cocker making a spectacle of himself in the middle of the muddy bog. Cocker is now almost half man, half mud, with his green woolly socks a magnet for the heavy clay.

Why he chooses to aim straight for the wettest and deepest part of the path is a mystery to all. A thought no doubt coming from the same part of his brain that told him to buy sandals instead of sturdy waterproof boots. It's painful to even watch him as he eventually grinds to a halt with the mud at his knees, panting for breath. He rests for a moment, wiping the sweat from his brow, then suddenly he bears down on his stick and gives a mighty push forward.

Whoosh. We both duck for cover as his bright-white foot shoots out of the ground like a rocket. Luckily the other foot anchors him down, or I fear that he may well have reached orbit.

Splosh! He lands back down in the bog, and loud raucous laughter fills the valleys for miles around. Then more laughter ensues as Cocker tries to stand while looking like the short-circuiting android C-3PO from *Star Wars*.

A spectating Dutch girl jumps up and down on the spot, laughing and crying at the same time while holding her crotch and trying unsuccessfully not to piss herself as her classmates take pictures of the unfortunate incident. Luckily for Cocker, two stern graybeards plow into the mire and help him to stand. Then we all laugh again as he delves back into the mud bath to retrieve the remains of his sandal and at last a muddy sock. Then with another almighty effort he frees the other foot and retreats to the side of the path, sitting in the muddy grass, trying to piece it all back together again.

"Ayers Rock, Nepal, Pennine Way, and day three of the Camino de Santiago, the journey has come to an end for his shit sandals."

Suddenly, in a fit of rage, he throws the sole into the field and everyone cheers again—and again—as he then dives angrily into his pack, producing the gleaming white training shoes. Then like a crazed magician, he waves his finger and puts one shoe back in his pack, then one on his foot, and now he's ready.

A final cheer goes out on the trail as the dandy highwayman's gleaming white shoe sinks straight to the bottom of the sludge.

\* \* \* \*

In the hillside village of Zariquiegui the Dutch have regrouped, and the tall blonde girl has her hand on her crotch again, with tears running down her face. "Whoops!" she shrieks, kicking her leg into the air, reenacting the precise moment when foot, sock, and sandal all parted company. Everyone is laughing again, including me.

Up ahead is the famous Fountain of Denial—talking of which, I cannot deny the fact that I need to piss like ten horses.

Now, according to legend, an exhausted and parched pilgrim was tempted by the Devil, who offered to show him a spring to quench his thirst in return for denying his faith. The pilgrim resisted, and his staunchness was rewarded by the appearance of Saint James dressed as a pilgrim, who revealed the location of a spring and gave him water from a scallop shell. Maybe the Devil will turn up now and show me a pristine urinal with an attendant on hand with crisp white towels and a selection of designer aftershaves, if I renounce my faith.

He doesn't show, and eventually I find myself walking alone, my hangover almost sweated out of my system. As I near the shrouded summit, I hear strange whooshing noises coming from within the clouds, and I glimpse the large white propeller of a wind turbine, followed by iron cutouts of pilgrims on foot, on horseback, and some with donkeys.

At the summit a freezing wind blows up my wet, sweaty back, chilling me to the bone, and the Dutch students arrive, shattering the peace and prompting me to leave immediately

Just before the descent and out of the wind stands a small 1980s camper-van with a jolly rosy-cheeked fellow on board, reminding me of Captain Pugwash, an infamous old cartoon favorite from the 1970s A cardboard sign on a fold-up table says two-euro donation and foot massages. I don't mind the donation, but the thought of Pugwash massaging my feet is a vision I can well do without at this hour of the day. So I opt for just a coffee, half a packet of custard creams, and a scallop shell for luck.

\* \* \* \*

The stony descent is a total nightmare and I'm in agony again with my torn knee. Up ahead is a statue of the Virgin Mary. Maybe she can help me. I feel like praying but feel a fool. There's no way I'm kneeling in front of a statue in a field.

What? Am I religious all of a sudden?

Beyond the Virgin stands the small town of Uterga and it's time for lunch. Pilgrims gather in the café, blocking every possible thoroughfare. I see the rude Frenchmen sitting around a table all red faced, drinking big tankards of lager and smoking an array of cigarettes, cigars, and pipes.

A happy Frenchman from a different group holds out his belly.

"Now," he says, pushing it out. "Santiago." He laughs, holding it in.

"I hope so, mate. You and me both," I say, looking down at my Buddha beer belly.

Inside the café I almost choke to death on my sandwich as a flashback of Cocker's rocket foot makes me laugh over and over.

The sun finally breaks through the clouds, and I find myself walking with a French biker pilgrim wearing a Harley Davidson sweatshirt. Unfortunately, we get so engaged in conversation about motorcycles that we miss the yellow arrows and carry on right down the road to god knows where. A roar goes up from behind us as pilgrims shout for us to turn back. So we retrace our steps and eventually part company on yet another very hilly stretch.

On a stony track coming into Puente la Reina, the firm but pert bottom of a lone female makes slow progress. I see the quiver of each toned bottom cheek time after time through her tight shorts. So I hang back for a while to view such a fine sight, and then step up a gear to check out the front.

*"Hola, buen camino,"* I say as I pass by.

*"Hola,"* she says in a sexy Euro accent, smiling.

Was that a hint of German, French perhaps? What a cutie. I hope she's staying at the next hostel! This is more like it. *Yes!*

In the old Roman town of Puente la Reina the sun leaps from behind the clouds, making all things bright and beautiful once again, but right outside the church door, a bird lies dead, with its intestines spilled out over the pavement with flies buzzing all over it.

From the shade of the church porch I watch and listen as a fuzzy-haired woman asks one of the locals the whereabouts of the pilgrims' hostel. The local points back the way we came, so I follow her and catch up.

My polite *hola* is met with an impolite grunt, and I can tell by her accent that she's Australian and very rude and contradictory from the start. Probably the mother of the rude little bastard I met yesterday, knowing my luck. As we approach the pilgrims shelter I see Swiss John loitering around the doorway.

*"¡Hola!"* he shrieks at the top of his voice. He's delighted to see me and announces that Belen and Cocker are staying here too.

"Fantastic!" I throw off my pack, remove my boots, and shake his hand.

We chat for a while until the Australian woman appears again. She is overjoyed to announce to me in her coarse, outback cattle-station voice, "Looks like I've taken the last bed mate." She lights a cigarette, smiling.

"For fuck's sakes!"

Swiss John excitedly begins to direct me to the hostel on

the other side of town, but after what happened at Larrasoaña, I'm not taking the word of the bush-tucking old bag. So I have a quick look around, but sure enough, it does look like all the beds are taken. Then Tucker appears from up the stairs.

"Hey, where are you going, dude?"

"No beds left," I say despairingly.

"Hello!" he shouts. "There are three empty rooms up here!"

Two minutes later I'm sitting and grinning beside my new bed in an empty and spacious dormitory, with me at one end and Tucker the other.

I remind myself for the second time in two days to beware of false prophets in the form of obnoxious pilgrims.

The bedroom window looks out onto a large garden with a drying area for clothes. Behind it, a disused factory chimney with what looks like some kind of dinosaur bird nest perched on top. I've never seen anything quite like it before. Now what shall I do for the afternoon? Definitely no more theme bars or police stations. In fact, after yesterday's shenanigans, I could do with an alcohol-free day.

I begin by taking a leisurely hot shower. Then I wash my boots and muddy clothes at the nearby fountain.

I feel almost human again and get chatting to the tall Dutch girl from earlier, who's washing her undercrackers at the sink. Then I get harassed and poked by an ancient French lady blaming me over someone else's washing in her way.

With all my jobs and ablutions done, it's time to respect a centuries-old tradition of afternoon siesta, so I head back to the room. But I should have known better.

A pillow flies across the landing, followed by a shrieking Dutch teen.

I watch in dismay as she picks it up and charges, screaming back into what was a nice, quiet dorm.

The youths have taken over, and bang goes my siesta!

Undeterred, I grab my roll mat and pilgrims' guide and go out onto the lawn for a sunbathe, snooze, and siesta. But no sooner do I set myself up than the youths arrive en masse and start throwing a Frisbee.

A Frisbee that looks remarkably like the one I left in Larrasoaña! I'm soon joined by Cocker, Tucker, and Swiss John, who persuades Cocker to let him give him a reflexology foot massage. It looks a painful affair and Cocker is yelping like a fanny.

"Dude, did you find a boot shop yet?" Tucker grins.

"No, I'm going to get another pair of sandals," Cocker says.

"Noooo!" we all say together.

"Don't be so stupid," I protest.

"Or you could just get *one*, dude." Tucker laughs.

"I was wondering about doing that, actually," says Cocker seriously.

"It was a joke, man." Tucker shakes his head.

"Or you could find the Spanish girl, and she can take you," says Swiss John. This idea appeals to Cocker the most by the look on his face.

"Yes, maybe I'll do that!" he says, with his eyes lit up.

It's a beautiful afternoon in Puente la Reina, and we all look up to see a Frisbee flying through the air, followed by the Dutch girls running onto the grass in their swimwear. The Dutch boys are lying facedown on the grass, watching the girls more than the Frisbee. Invisible clouds of teenage sexual tension float through the air at the sight of seminaked female flesh, bending, wobbling, and rolling about with their legs akimbo. Our group has gone strangely quiet too.

"*Tjonger, tjonger,* and *tjonger,*" I say, wiping my brow.

The Dutch boys look up and laugh.

"Dude, what does that mean?" asks Tucker.

"It's Dutch for, oh boy, oh boy, and oh boy!" I tell them.

I shut my eyes and drift off to the sounds of girls' cheeky laughter and Tucker's *tjonger, tjonger, tjonger*ing. I drift a bit more to girls' laughter and finally into a Dutch hard-core porn dream involving naked girls and a Frisbee.

"Ahhh, my arse!" I scream, leaping up from the ground as a large, angry red ant falls from my shorts.

"The little red bastard has scored a bull's-eye right on my—"

"*Tjonger, tjonger, tjonger,*" says Cocker, laughing along with all the Dutch youths.

"Yeah, very funny, thank you." I skulk off back to the room and apply some after-bite to my ringing sting.

I return to find the guys with their books out. Cocker reads *The Pilgrimage* by Pablo Coolio. Tucker reads the *Darwin Awards* and Swiss John is reading *Dope Stories* by Howard Marks.

"That book by Pablo Coolio—is he that drugs baron?" I ask Cocker.

"No, that's my book," says Swiss John.

Cocker sighs. "Paulo Coelho is his name. You wouldn't like it, and if you must know, he's a guru, not a drug lord or whatever you think."

"What the fuck is a guru, and how do you know I won't like it?"

Cocker pulls a sour face and hides in his silly little book as I read from my professional pilgrims' guide.

Today's episode says,

In the Church of San Pedro Apostle here in Puente la Reina, the image of a bird is worshipped. Legend has it that when the statue was kept in a small chapel in the middle of the bridge, a little bird used to go and clean the Virgin's face every day, which was seen as a good sign by the local community.

But what about the dead bird outside the church I saw earlier?

What kind of sign is that? Is it a sign for me, I wonder? It's definitely not a good sign, that's for sure!

Belen appears, looking bright and beautiful, smelling fresh and exciting.

"Would you like to join us?" asks Cocker, getting up and offering his chair like a dapper gent.

"No, the town is open now. I go for shopping," she replies softly.

"Oh, what are you buying?" asks overtly enthusiastic Cocker.

"Erm, err . . ." She looks funny all of a sudden, not knowing the English word for it while we wait for an answer.

"You know, erm, ladies' things, err, ladies' time." She shrugs, red faced.

At once, three heads turn back to book reading and one head goes into town with Belen to buy ladies' things and new boots (we hope).

The happy shoppers return a few hours later with happy, smiling faces.

I reckon Cocker must have coaxed her into a bar for a few

drinks, as they both look a little flushed, and he looks very pleased with himself in more ways than one. His brand-new pair of beaming boots are indeed a sight to behold, and Belen offers us all an apple as we study his new footwear.

"Dude, are they Gore-Tex?" says Tucker, prodding and squeezing.

"Never mind that. Are they even leather?" wonders Swiss John.

"How much did you pay for them?" I ask him.

"Eighty euro," he says.

"Wow, they definitely saw you coming then." I laugh.

"And they definitely will see him coming now," scoffs Swiss John.

"But they are so comfortable and light," says Cocker.

"Cocker and his Technicolor dream boots," I joke.

* * * *

As the night closes in on Puente la Reina, a group of pilgrim musicians gather outside the hostel, drinking wine and singing South American love songs. The Austrian guy I met this morning sings "Wish You Were Here" by Pink Floyd, as the Brazilian Afro guy beats out a funky rhythm on a small drum. It has all the makings of a good little party, but as with the other hostels, we all have to be in by 10:00 p.m., lest there be any ill behavior, I suppose. Tucker and I go back to our room and stumble upon some more quality entertainment in the form of the sight and sound of girls prancing around in their underwear while doing girlish things with powders and creams. The boys lie facedown on their beds with their eyes on stalks, trying with difficulty to suppress a lifetime of pent-up sexual tension. It's hard to know where to look, so I stick my head straight into my book, as does Tucker at the other end of the room, and we communicate only by using our eyes and eyebrows, frequently peeping out over our books for a quick perv.

One of the girls looks out the window and screams, signaling for her friends, and my heart misses a beat as ten nubile girls bend over at the window in an array of G-string lingerie, laughing, giggling, and wobbling at two familiar figures behaving very strangely on the grass below. Eventually I get up and see what all the fuss is about. On the lawn below us, we see Swiss John and Cocker crouching down on the ground, then rising slowly with their arms in the air, chanting some wacky mantra with their eyes closed.

"What are you doing down there, you clowns?" I shout.

"We're pretending to be seeds," shouts Cocker, pointing to his Pablo Coolio book laid out on the grass.

"Are you guys high or something?" laughs one of the girls.

"No, we're pretending to be seeds. Why don't you join us?" shouts Swiss John, arms outstretched like some kind of messiah.

"What are they doing down there?" Tucker yawns, rubbing his eyes.

"Pretending to be seeds?" I reply.

"Dude, those guys are nuts," he says, shaking his head.

"No, seeds!"

Tucker's beady eyes keep peeping over the top of his book as one of the girls bends over to take her socks off, giving us a full view of her undercarriage. Another girl removes her T-shirt altogether to reveal a small but firm pair of breasts as a strange man walks into the room. Tucker and I exchange worried looks as the little guy takes off his shirt, drops his trousers, and sets off strutting round the room like a banty cockerel wearing only a leopard-skin posing pouch.

What on earth is going on here?

*Who the fuck is this?* I mouth to Tucker.

*Dunno,* he shrugs back.

Now the guy is talking to the boys and the half-naked girls. I wonder if I ought to say something, but they don't run away, so I can only figure that he must be their teacher and not some pervert who's wandered in off the street.

I'd often wondered who was in charge of this lot.

"Another mystery solved."

I climb into my still-damp sleeping bag as a G-stringed girl to the side of me climbs up to her bunk like a clumsy baby giraffe.

I look the other way but come face-to-face with the crotch and bouncing breasts of another girl, failing miserably to jump onto the bed above me.

Then, as if by magic, the lights suddenly go out and the room falls silent. I hear the youth across from me scratching an insect bite, and then someone down the room farts a little tune.

*"Tjonger, tjonger, tjonger,"* joke the youths as the place erupts into laughter. I hear the kinky teacher shushing them up as the squeaking and scratching gets louder and faster to a chorus of girly giggles.

Then the penny drops. The youth is masturbating frantically for all he's worth.

Oh well, as the saying goes, *If you can't beat 'em . . .*

# TECHNICOLOR DREAM BOOTS

THE NEXT MORNING TUCKER and I pass the ominous decaying bird, and somewhere from the galaxy I get an overwhelming feeling of doom, a special something reserved just for me.

"How the fuck can you walk the Camino de Santiago in G-string underpants?" I ask Tucker.

"Dude, I got abrasion just thinking about it!"

\* \* \* \*

In the ancient village of Cirauqui we spot the boots before we spot the owner, Lord Cocker. He is sprawled out in the street like some kind of Roman emperor as Belen feeds him olives and grapes while fanning his grinning face with a huge leaf.

"How's it going? How goes the new footwear?" I ask him.

He looks up and bangs them on the cobbles, showing off their robust qualities.

"They are just great, so light and comfortable," he chirps, like he's in some kind of walking-boot commercial.

I'm still not convinced, though. I reckon in a few days he'll be walking like an Egyptian.

I sit with them awhile as Tucker disappears into the distance and I read what medieval French pilgrim Aymeric Picaud has to say about this area.

> Take care not to drink the water here, neither yourself nor your horse, for it is a deadly river! On the way to Santiago we came across two Navarrese sitting by the bank, sharpening the knives they use to flay pilgrims' horses which had drunk the water and died. We asked them if the water was fit to drink, and they lying replied that it was, whereupon we gave it to our horses to drink. Two of them dropped dead at once and the Navarrese flayed them there and then.

Hard times for poor-old Aymeric.

Belen invites me to join them in some traditional Spanish food: crusty bocadillos with nice soft cheese and chorizo, gorgeous ham, and large misshapen tomatoes, green and red in color, with a melt-in-your-mouth taste. I could happily sit here all day long but the urge to continue is strong, so I leave the young lovers to their blossoming courtship and march on. Eventually I find myself walking next to a beautiful green river, and finally I cross over a lovely old bridge into the beautiful town of Estella. It hasn't been a long walk today, but with every single step comes pain, starting at my feet and moving to my knee via my back and ever painful ribs and on occasion coming out of my mouth via terrible expletives.

As per usual the queue to get in the hostel is mobbed with rude pilgrims. As the doors open, they stampede in with packs on, and a young Italian boy is almost trampled to death.

* * * *

Today is Friday, traditionally the day where the working man puts down his tools and drinks beer to celebrate the start of the weekend. In the grand plaza I sit alone with a large glass of wine to fortify me before my shopping trip to the chemist, as it's bound to end up with some kind of stressful Euro confusion.

It's a lovely day to sit and people-watch from behind my sunglasses, with plenty of women to report. Unfortunately, none of the nubile variety, only heavily-made-up mothers smoking lipstick-stained white cigarettes while drinking wine and coffee in garish outfits dragged down by heavy jewelry.

I spot the rude Frenchmen at a café across the way, drinking tankards of lager in the hot sun. They all look sunburned to hell.

Maybe someone should tell them to apply sun cream and not to drink beer, smoke fags, and eat frogs and whatnot. See what they say?

The kinky Dutch teacher and one of the students appear and sit directly in front of me, not noticing me behind them. They laugh and joke like a pair of young lovers, and I deduce from their body language that the sly old dog might be giving her the bone.

I'm joined at my table by a worried-looking Swiss John.

"I can't get hold of my wife! It is most unusual!" he cries.

"Well, you know what they say. While the cat's away," I joke.

His poor face drops, and immediately I wish I hadn't said it, as it plunges him into deeper despair.

A drummer in full medieval costume walks into the plaza, banging and crashing away as the local children go crazy. Bang! A firework explodes, the drum suddenly stops, and playtime starts. Thankfully Swiss John is smiling again as he watches the children play. So I take the time to finish writing my crumpled postcards, paying particular attention to one for a very special friend back home. The picture on the front shows a man being savagely gored by a bull in Pamplona.

*Dear Fuck Face,*

*Wish you were here . . .*

*Getting gored by bulls*

*Love from Eddie Rock*

So with playtime over, we drink up and hit the streets, finding a chemist and a postbox. Then a steady walk back to the hostel with Swiss John confessing to me that he was partial to a bit of heroin in his younger days.

Back at the hostel we find Cocker and Belen on a top bunk, massaging each other's feet while staring dreamily into each other's eyes.

"Wine fountain tomorrow," says Cocker.

"I beg your pardon?"

"Yes. Wine fountain tomorrow," he says again.

"A wine fountain? Where? No, hang on, don't tell me . . . it's on chocolate mountain next to the beer waterfall."

"You'll see," says Cocker. "I thought it would be up your street!"

A wine fountain. Honestly, does he think I was born yesterday? I laugh.

In my mind I see a stately wine fountain with a muscular Neptune and Apollo, the birth of Venus with streams of wine flowing from the penises of cherubs—and Cocker with his mouth open, refreshing himself on vino blanco!

A Brazilian guy arrives in a taxi and climbs out onto a set of crutches with a cast on one foot. So I help him into the hostel and into the dorm with his pack. He tells me that he took a bad fall crossing the Pyrenees on day one and has ruptured his Achilles tendon. So from now on he will be taking each stage by taxi. There I was complaining about my back, knee, and ribs, but this poor man has come from Brazil, and on the morning of day one it's all over for the guy. He also tells me that *two* people died coming from Saint-Jean-Pied-de-Port, in the blizzard.

So I've got a lot to be thankful for, really.

\* \* \* \*

That evening, Tucker, Cocker, Belen, Swiss John, the crippled Brazilian, and I find a nice restaurant near the plaza, and all, bar one of us, has the eight-euro pilgrim's meal with free wine. Swiss John, however, spends twenty euros on a plate of six neatly arranged asparagus spears, with a dribble of sauce on top and no free wine.

So to change the subject from his extortionate meal, he decides yet again to tell us his theory of the Camino de Santiago Gospel according to Swiss John.

He tells us that the first 200 kilometers of the Camino represent our youth, when we are getting used to our environment and learning who and what we are in life.

The second 200 kilometers represent our adolescent years, when we are trying out new things (*Like ecstasy and heroin?* I wonder to myself) and doing wild and carefree things.

The third 200 kilometers are our adult lives, when we get down to the serious business of making a living and making our lives happen and have meaning.

The last 200 kilometers is our old age, when we reflect on where we have been and what we have done and how we want to end our lives.

(Still probably doing the odd ecstasy tablet now and again.)

The remaining kilometers are the walk to Finisterre on the Atlantic coast, and this represents our time after death, when the pain has ended.

"Life is pain," says Swiss John.

"Sounds like he's been reading too much Pablo Coolio again." I laugh.

"Paulo Coelho is his name," says Cocker in a huff.

"So what was that tree-growing bullshit all about then?"

"Dudes, have you been overdoing it on the acid?" laughs Tucker.

"No, no, no, it was our way of regrowth and new beginning," says the sagely Swiss John.

"What a load of bollocks!" I tell them.

"It's not bollocks!" Cocker protests. "Once we master the

seed exercise, we are moving on to the speed exercise," he says, pulling a silly face.

"See, I knew it was something to do with drugs. Pablo Cocker!"

"Oh yes, har, har, very funny," he says. "It's actually where you walk along at half the speed as normal while taking in your surroundings."

"What's new? You do that anyway," I tell him.

With the meal over and the wine quaffed, we toddle off back to the hostel, and even before the lights go out, the snoring starts and my imagination takes me back to the scene in the Vietnam movie *Full Metal Jacket*, when they throw a bedsheet over the fat snoring soldier, then pull it tight, and the whole platoon takes turns bashing the fuck out of him with their soaps in their socks. Now there's a thought!

# THE WINE FOUNTAIN

ONLY IN THE DREAMS OF HOMER J. SIMPSON would you expect to see a wine fountain. But it seems it does exist after all, so I'm up early. It's 5:00 a.m. and Manuel and Swiss John are standing around the doorway like a pair of knob-heads, waiting for the hostelero to let them out. Our three-euro breakfast is more like a chimpanzee's tea party but with far less manners, hygiene, and patience. As we begin to eat, vulture-eyed pilgrims gather around the outskirts of the table, waiting impatiently for a seat to become available—a bit like a game of musical chairs at a children's birthday party, only twice as daft. Because as soon as a chair is vacant, even for a split second, it immediately has a new owner; then another idiotic Euro debate as the chair is tugged backward and forward, just like you'd see at a four-year-old child's birthday party.

"What is wrong with some people?"

I need a fresh coffee, so I leave my plate on my chair to signify to someone that the chair is taken, and two seconds later the toast is stuck to the big fat arse of a stupid Frenchwoman.

"Nice one, thank you," I say.

"Look at my trousers!" she shrieks.

"Look at my toast; you've flattened it." I point to her big fat arse.

"You are a rude man," she says.

"Yes, I know," I tell her.

As she waddles off, another rude pilgrim seizes the moment and now he's sat in my chair next to my hot coffee and plate.

"For fuck's sake, man!"

After breakfast, we gather outside in the cool morning and watch our own Romeo and Juliet getting ready for the day.

"Why do you keep calling her *bellend*?" I taunt Cocker, who's trying his hardest not to stare at her mesmerizing bosoms, enhanced even more by the Wonderbra effects of the pack straps.

"No, Belen—a bit like Helen, but with a *B*," he says.

"Sounds like *bellend* to me."

"Dude, what's a *bellend*?" asks Tucker.

"It's the end of your penis," I tell him. "'Cause it's shaped like a bell."

As Belen adjusts her funbags, her tiny water bottle hits the cobbles with the lid snapping clean off. She stifles a sob at the symbol of their shared love lying shattered and broken at their feet.

"Maybe we could glue it," says Cocker, clutching the remains.

"Behave yourself. Look at the state of it," I tell him.

Belen sobs and Cocker hugs her, wiping away her tears. Then, as she stops crying, he tries in vain to mend it with some superglue from an old tobacco tin out of his pack.

"That's not going to work, you flaming tool," I tell him again, and what makes it worse is the useless cockend doesn't even have his own water bottle. He used mine for the first day or so and then Belen's, and now that he can't mend this one, it looks like he's going to cry too.

"Oh for fuck's sake, here, have one of mine," I say, lending them one of my adventure-sized unbreakable bottles.

We all set off happily for a short while until our pace gets slower and slower.

"Yeah, I get it, two's company and three's a crowd."

"What?" says Cocker, acting dumb.

"Have you started your speed exercise this morning?" I ask him.

\* \* \* \*

Up ahead Manuel stands at a fork in the road, happily telling everyone that the wine fountain is closed. Where on earth he's got this information from at this hour of the day is anybody's guess, but I'm not taking the word of a Jonah when it comes to the nitty-gritty of wine-fountain enjoyment. Upon my arrival, I'm disappointed to report that the fountain is not like the one I had imagined at all. There are no jets of wine firing into the air, no cherubs or bare-breasted mermaids or anything; it quite simply comes out a tap, and contrary to the belief of Manuel, it is open for business. "You'd never get this in England," I say to a bemused Japanese tourist as I empty my water onto the ground, replacing it with cool, fresh wine and take a large hearty gulp. "Mmm, fresh vino." Very nice indeed.

Tucker arrives, complaining about the snoring last night, and a few people I've never seen before pitch camp and hit the vino too. It would have been great craic if the Afro lads were here with their guitars and drums, and I wish I had never given my other bottle to Belen now.

"Free wine on tap. You wouldn't get this in England!" I shout to Tucker.

"Bloody good job, the country would be on its knees," says one of the new English pilgrims, and I have to agree that this is the best morning of free entertainment since Cocker lost his sandal, and talk of the devil.

"Here he is, Mr. Skip the light fandango and his neon rubber boots. . . . We were just talking about you."

"All good, I hope," says Cocker, looking concerned.

"Of course," I say angelically.

"Whoa, not bad for free wine," he gasps.

Belen declines, saying it is too early, and she sits with us and peels an orange, drifting off into her thoughts.

"Do you mind if I join you?" asks the English pilgrim.

"Not at all; the more the merrier," I tell him.

"Hi, everybody. My name is Joe," he says.

"Joe, this is Cocker and this is Bellend," I tell him.

Joe coughs and splutters wine straight out of his nose while trying to speak, and Cocker gives me a dirty look. Belen looks up from her book

"B. E. L. E. N.," Cocker retorts like an infant.

He eventually calms down and gets into the party mood.

"Come on, Cocker, make the most of it! Get plenty in you, mate!"

I thrust the bottle into his hand, but Belen is anxious to

leave now, so we take a few pictures of our group and then Belen gets up and throws on her pack, only just managing to squeeze her huge knockers between the pack straps. Her boobs appear to be getting bigger every day!

"I'm going, boys. Enjoy your fun," she says, and we all watch her cute little ass wiggle slowly out of sight. Now Cocker is stuck between a rock and a hard place, but like the big Jesse he is, he chooses love over alcohol and runs off up the road.

"*¡Adiós, amigos¡*" he shouts, running after Belen.

"Love is the drug," sighs Joe thoughtfully as Cocker turns and gives us the finger.

"Pussy-whipped and he's only just met her." I sigh.

A group of very stern-looking French pilgrims arrives, and even in French it's easy to understand what they are saying, and it's not friendly. They fill their canteens with water, take boring photos, and leave us with very dirty looks. One of them is the hippo-arsed breakfast-flattening madam in a fresh pair of shorts. She casts me a filthy glare, but all I can do is laugh. A solitary nun walks past, crossing herself and looking to the heavens, as do a couple of old Spanish ladies in black knitted cardigans, only adding to the hilarity. The Dutch students arrive with noise levels reaching epidemic.

Today for some reason they all have red T-shirts on with the words "Camino 2003 TRUE SURVIVORS" and their names underneath.

There's DIRK, JOOP, FRANZ, BERT, LEO, HENNIE, JAN, JOYCE, and JAAP.

The kid Dirk, he's the one with the squeaking bed.

"Hey, Dirk! Geen masturbatie meer alsjeblieft" " I shout across, and give him the universal wanker sign. Dirk looks sheepish, with his friends laughing and wanker signing, while rolling huge cigarettes of pouch tobacco and taking crafty swigs of wine before their gimp of a teacher turns up in his leopard-skin underpants.

"Can you honestly imagine a wine fountain in England?" I ask Joe.

"It would make a good documentary." He laughs.

*This week on* Wine Fountain UK.

*Police officers John and Mike are back at the wine fountain as tension flares between rival gangs. Fountain security guard Bill is finally released from hospital two weeks after his vicious assault, while tramps Percy and Lawrence have an unpleasant surprise when wine turns to water. Stay tuned for this week's episode of* Wine Fountain UK.

I bid farewell to Joe and wobble along the strange road. It's getting very hot, and odd buzzing feelings have started in my feet. Suddenly my whole body starts to itch. When I sit, I want to stand. When I stand, I want to sit. The back of my hands and ears are getting covered in some kind of small itchy blisters, so I rip the sleeves from a long-sleeved shirt to make some sun protection and catch my reflection in a window. I look like something off *Mad Max*, and the wine is taking its toll on my senses.

"Ooooh the sun has got his hat on, hip hip hooray, the sun has got his hat on and he's coming out to play! Oh the sun has got." What the fuck, I can't get this stupid song out of my head. It goes around and around on a continuous loop. What depth of my subconscious has it come from? Not that I'm complaining, you see . . . as I'm afraid, I'm very, very drunk. Wine for breakfast. "Rock and roll." All I need now is sex and drugs and—"Yeehar!" Maybe the Dutch youths really have got some weed?

Or maybe Swiss John has got some E?

I find myself ambling along, staring at the ground and wobbling from side to side while trying to step over the ant trails that cross the path every three meters or so. Tiny little lines of movement I don't want to stand in. I must not kill an ant! It will bring me bad karma. I once saw a documentary on an Indian yogi on a Hindu pilgrimage. He just rolled and rolled along the ground with his disciples in front of him, sweeping his path so he didn't kill any insects. Mind you, the silly bastard almost got run over by a lorry. Suddenly I find myself lost and alone in the middle of a field, looking and feeling like some kind of scarecrow, so I retrace my steps and finally notice a yellow arrow and proceed with caution on this very hot drunken day.

Luckily, up ahead I notice the camper-van with Pugwash at the helm, so I have four mugs of coffee in the hope it will sober me up, and I manage to bum a cigarette from smoking angel Benny. I get chatting a bit with Pugwash, and he tells me he walked the Camino when he retired from the navy and returns every year to provide pilgrims with coffee, biscuits, and foot massages. I still don't fancy a foot massage but his coffee ain't too bad.

* * * *

Back on the trail there's not a soul in sight, so I try to play a few tunes on the harmonica. So here goes! I try *The Great Escape* theme and "Dirty Old Town"—a song by the Pogues that I tried to learn in Canada without success. The theme tune to *The Waltons* is impossible, but before the hour I have "The Great Escape" almost to a tee. Two angry, red-faced Dutch ladies emerge from the wheat fields. "Oops!" Looks like I've ruined their siesta and they are cursing me in Dutch. I lived in Holland for many years, so I half understand their language and they call me "a prick" and a "ball bag" and other unsavory Dutch words, including the C word.

Now, why couldn't they have been a couple of twentysomething Dutch ladies, preferably one blonde and one brunette laid in the field, having sexual fantasies about a lone harmonica-learning hiker.

Now that's more like it.

The sun beats down ferociously as I arrive in the small town of Sansol. The hostel is down a steep hill, and my knee almost pops out of its socket yet again, then back up another steep hill until I finally arrive in the one-horse town of Torres del Río. I spot Tucker sunbathing happily in the plaza and drinking the rest of his wine. He's first in line for the hostel and I'm proudly second. So I nip to the shop for a six-pack of beer and some cigarettes to while away the time. A Dutch lady called Whilamena joins us, and we all enjoy the world's most ice-cold, refreshing beer.

More pilgrims arrive, including Manuel wearing a thick woolly jumper and complaining that it's too cold, and the Dutch harmonica-appreciation society join the queue, still complaining of their ruined siesta.

Our peaceful gathering soon comes to an abrupt halt as a group of rude, obnoxious pilgrims turns up, and our queuing system, if there ever was one, goes straight out the window.

When the shocked little Spanish lady arrives with a key, the place descends into total chaos. Tucker and I look on in disbelief at yet another display of Euro lunacy, but our friend Whilamena is angry and is gonna do something about it. She is rightfully third in line and pushes through to her place as a tall Italian man is jolted backward onto her bare foot! Poor-old Whilamena. She jumps around on one leg, holding her toe while screaming in pain, but the tall guy doesn't even apologize. He just looks all deadpan with cold fish eyes, like they do, pretending it hasn't happened! So she gives him a big shove in the back and he still doesn't respond. So she pinches him hard on his arm like an angry child to no response yet again, then limps her way into the hostel.

To try and avoid this kind of infantile pilgrim behavior, Tucker and I have quickly invented a new policy of checking our guidebooks to find out how many beds there are, then count how many people there are, and if it all adds up, we sit back and watch the carnage unfold before our eyes. Eventually the commotion dies down and we saunter indoors unflustered, and I wonder to myself again what all the fuss was about.

* * * *

It's time for another earplugged siesta for Eduardo in the upstairs dorm. I wake up an hour or so later to the sounds of alarmingly loud angelic singing as the Dutch harmonica appreciation society ladies rearrange their beds in an attempt to get their own back on me. They can actually sing quite well, and I find it therapeutic, lying there humming along.

A Welsh family arrives with their four children, a girl of around twelve years, two younger children of about seven or eight, and a small boy of around six. It's taken them a month to get to here already, but fair play to them. God loves a trier! That's what I keep telling myself anyway, so I venture out into the bright lights of Torres del Río and find a nice restaurant situated in a lovely old stone building. I sit up at the bar to enjoy another cold, refreshing beer served by a jolly little man wearing an array of trinkets, with rings on every finger and bells on his toes by the sounds of things. A beautiful woman emerges from the kitchen with jet-black hair and piercing eyes, carrying plates of gorgeous-smelling food. Broomsticks and five-pointed stars hang all around, and I'm beginning to wonder if the woman is some kind of sexy witch, as she's certainly cast a spell on me, that's for sure.

I notice both she and the fellow are wearing five-pointed stars around their necks. Perhaps they are Wiccans or pagans, maybe? We start talking about Ireland and the mythical places like Newgrange and Stonehenge in Britain. The little man comes over and starts chatting. They both speak very good English and are good people. Manuel enters the bar with a couple of ladies he's met on the trail. One lady is Australian and her name is Jan. The other lady is English and her name is Sarah. Sarah tells me that I remind her of her son.

"Must be a good-looking chap then," I joke.

We dine on succulent lamb and roast potatoes, and Manuel, who is watching his figure, gives me one of his chops with some potatoes. He is keen to point out with negative joviality that it will probably take the Welsh family six months to walk the Camino de Santiago, having already taken a month to get here. He checks his step counter and announces that he has walked 19,784 steps today and he reckons that we will all walk well over a million steps.

"And feel every one of them, I should imagine," I add painfully.

Back at the hostel, the snoring is to behold. I'm thankful for my earplugs. I nip for a slash in the middle of the night and see poor-old Tucker wide awake, reading his book with his headlamp. He doesn't look happy. To make matters worse, the loudest snorers are usually the rudest people, making them totally abysmal human beings. Many people are awake, including all of the little Welsh children, and their mother comforts the youngest child, who is crying. I drift off to sleep, fantasizing about doing the rounds with a pillow and small-caliber pistol with silencer.

# L●VE ●N THE R●CKS

FOUR VERY RUDE, RED-FACED OVERWEIGHT PILGRIMS look very refreshed this morning, and about thirty others look absolutely shattered.

My feet are now blocks of pain, and my whole body itches to the song that goes, "Jessie, paint your pictures 'bout how it's gonna be," only the name Jessie has been replaced by the name Cocker, and yet another idiotic song plays over and over in my jumbled mind:

*"Old woman, old woman, are you fond of dancing?"*

*"Yes, sir, yes, sir, I am fond of dancing."*

To ease the loop of loony songs, I plow on with the harmonica and *The Great Escape* theme tune. Over and over I play as my pace quickens with all my problems at the back of my mind, like some kind of marching musical meditation.

The theme tune to *The Waltons* is quite a difficult one. As is "Waltzing Matilda." "Hitler Has Only Got One Ball" is easy, but "He Ain't Heavy, He's My Brother" is far too hard, and Stevie Wonder's harmonica solo in the Eurythmics' "There Must Be an Angel" is totally impossible. So it's back to *The Great Escape* and the theme tune to *The A-Team*.

Up ahead two Japanese pilgrims negotiate a small stream. The woman skips over the stones with ease and stands, shouting instructions as the man launches himself like a mountain goat onto a dangerous peaked rock and stands there balancing, strangely staring into space. I run to save him in case he falls backward but suddenly he leaps forward onto another rock, balances for a few seconds, then jumps safely to solid ground. He made it and we're all laughing!

* * * *

A few miles down the road I come to rest at a terraced café in the beautiful town of Viana. I'm joined at the table by Jan, the Australian, and English Sarah, who speaks very posh and keeps telling me I remind her of her son.

"Lucky him," I tell her with a hint of sarcasm.

"Isn't this a lovely place," says Jan, looking around the beautiful medieval plaza, illuminated to full architectural glory by the early-morning sun.

"Beats a Sunday morning in Scunthorpe." I laugh.

"Where's Scunthorpe?" asks Jan. "It sounds a bladdy awful place."

"It's up north," says Sarah, mimicking a northern accent. "And there's a joke by John Cooper Clarke," she says, with a glint in her eye. "Who put the *cunt* in Scunthorpe?"

"Was it the same bloke who put the *Grim* in Grimsby and the ming in Immingham?" I joke

"I don't think I ever want to go there," says Jan.

All three of us shake our heads at the same time, and the Japanese couple joins us at the table. I notice that the man is blind, and at once I'm ashamed of myself for moaning about my little problems when they are nothing compared to his. After strong coffee I march onward and another mystery solved yet again.

"Who did put the *cunt* in Scunthorpe?"

I'd always thought you just crossed the *S* out.

While passing a church, I bump straight into an overly enthusiastic Benny, the clean angel exiting the beautiful building while staring up at the facade. *"Estupendo, estupendo,"* he keeps saying, looking to the sky instead of where he's going, and still immaculately attired.

I wish I could say the same. Normally the churches en route are locked up, but this one is open, and nice and cool inside, so I have another go at praying, and the same words echo round my brain.

"The Lord helps those who help themselves." All I can think of are the bad things I have done in my life and all the people I've hurt by my actions, with normally myself coming out the worst of all in the end. I can feel impending doom on the horizon and wonder yet again what I'm doing with my life and the reasons for doing this Camino, and what I'll do when it's over. The thought of going back to Scunthorpe fills me with dread. There has to be an answer. I cheer myself up by sticking a couple of euros in the magic candle box, and five little candles light up. There we go, five sins forgiven?

A blast of devilishly hot air hits me as I leave the cool sanctuary, and today every bit of me hurts. I have blisters on top of blisters, and the ant bite on my ring piece is driving me crazy. Maybe God is punishing me for watching too much porn or smoking too much dope?

On the entrance to Logroño cemetery the inscription on the wall catches my eye and I translate with Franklin.

"'I was once as you are and you will be what I am.'"

"In other words, dead!"

I'm not sure I like the Spanish graveyards one bit. I don't want to be bricked up in a wall when I die; I'm claustrophobic at the best of times. I cross the Río Ebro and pass a group of men fishing from the famous bridge. Outside the hostel, Manuel is complaining that his antique backpack is rubbing his shoulders to the bone, so Whilamena steps in and offers him a couple of sanitary towels to use as padding. I grimace as Manuel then tapes them to his shoulder straps and tries them for comfort with a big smile on his face.

The sun is fierce, so I move across to the shade of the four-story building opposite the church to watch a Spanish wedding unfold.

I have a terrible urge to scratch a very intimate insect bite in a terribly awkward place, and I'm in no position to give it the scratch it severely warrants. I leap up to go scratch and . . . *bang!* A plant pot smashes next to my pack, followed a second later by . . . *smash!* A child's plastic toy. And four stories up, I spy a sorry little face peeping over the balcony. Saved by an ant bite. It must have been heaven sent?

As usual, there's an unruly queue to get in the hostel, and as soon as the doors open all hell breaks loose. Luckily, I end up getting a bottom bunk in the claustrophobic boxy bunk beds, pretty similar to the graveyard, really, but less spacious. So I climb into my cask and pop in my plugs for a siesta. I open my eyes and pull open my towel curtain and come, face-to-arse, with a cycling man's bare bottom.

"Fuck sake!" Talk about being rudely awakened. I fall back into my coffin and stare at the graffiti on the bunk above. I hear Swiss John and two Dutch men babbling on about shaving their legs.

"We like to shave down below. It stops any chafing," says one.

"Yes, we do like to shave down there. It makes it nice and soft, you know," says the other.

"When I'm at home," says Swiss John, "I like to shave my balls. It makes them nice and soft too. My wife, she really likes it."

"Yes, it makes them playful," says the Dutch man. "We like it too."

"Elton John shaves his too. I saw it on the TV," says the other cyclist.

I can't believe what I'm hearing. I need to get out of this place, quick!

I meet Cocker queuing for the showers, staring sadly at the ground, not even managing a smile for his old friend.

"What's up with you? Cut your ball bag shaving?" I ask him.

"No, Belen's boyfriend is here!"

"What!"

In the plaza, two very sad heads are deep in conversation, and it doesn't look like it's going particularly well. Poor Belen looks very upset.

"I thought you said her boyfriend has turned up?" I say to Cocker.

"That's him," he moans.

"Holy Jesus! I was expecting to see some kind of Ricky Martin or Enrique Iglesias type boyfriend in a Porsche 911 or something, not cardigan-wearing Julio Iglesias in a Citroën 2CV. "He must be about fifty," I point out.

"He's fifty-one," sighs Cocker, "and she's twenty-nine."

We sit on a table, out of earshot, and weigh up the situation.

"He doesn't look like he's got a lot of go in him, does he? I can't imagine him getting her on all fours and giving her a good banging all night long, can you?" I ask him.

Cocker's face drops. "Do you have to be so vulgar?"

"Err, yes I do! Look at what's going on here, man. That girl is in serious need of a good fucking, and look who she's got to do it with. Stop beating around the bush and get in there, son!"

As Cocker stands up to buy the beers, Belen looks up and they exchange nervous little smiles. Suddenly, Julio stands abruptly, then turns and leaves without so much as a kiss or a kind word, and it looks to me like Belen has just given old Julio the Spanish archer—"the el bow." But now poor-old Belen is in a state, and who better to do the comforting than my amigo Cocker returning with the beers. I leave them to it and return to the hostel.

Back in the room an enormous fat woman has miraculously squeezed herself into her coffin and the gay cyclists loiter with intent, cruising the bedrooms in their skin-tight biking shorts. A pretty but odd American woman changes into a silk nightshirt, and her boyfriend puts on his silk PJs.

At 3:00 a.m., I wake up, screaming, while dreaming that I was being buried in a wall in a Spanish cemetery, and then I scream even louder as I'm comforted by a naked Dutch man.

# WHATEVER NEXT?

I START OUT EARLY WITH YANNIK, a big Danish fellow. He has the most impressive Viking beard I've ever seen. He tells me he started to grow it back in Le Puy, over a thousand kilometers back. The streets here are an awesome spectacle with so many lovely buildings, fountains, and statues. Maybe I should just stay in Spain after the Camino. Maybe get a camper-van like Pugwash and try to stay below the radar. Every time I think of Scunthorpe I feel hopelessly depressed and wonder what I'm going to do when I finish. We pop into a café and have a nice cup of coffee and then I realize I've lost my wallet. So I run back quickly, hoping for the best but also planning for the worst, while foolishly getting a cod liver oil tablet lodged in my dry throat, which then melts and leaves me burping horrible cod liver breath all the way back to the hostel. One idiotically excitable graybeard tells me I'm going the wrong way as I come face-to-face with him in the narrow streets.

Back to the hostel, I find my wallet where I left it, underneath my pillow, and walk out of town relieved. But it doesn't last long, as I feel a huge cold sore building up on my bottom lip. That's all I need right now! A facial sore to go with all the rest of them. Great!

I wonder how Cocker's getting on. I haven't seen him this morning, but he'll be there somewhere, ambling along slowly with Belen and hopefully putting in some serious groundwork now with Julio out of the picture. It's hot, hot, hot, and my heat rash is growing and spreading daily, now finding its way onto my lower back where my pack has been rubbing. The approach into Nájera is uninspiring, and at a rusty old bridge the arrows completely disappear!

*Which way now?* I wonder.

The midday sun is taking its toll, so I go with my instincts and end up walking half an hour in completely the wrong direction, ending up at a solitary farm. A fat man in a dirty egg- and wine-stained vest points me back the way I came. Sweltering heat waves rise from the road and I watch as a miniature Clint Eastwood figure approaches me with his poncho blowing in the wind. When he's at my side, he stands about four feet tall. Mini Clint speaks Spanish and has a quick word with the dirty fat man and we both walk back together in total silence.

I leave him staring at a wall with some pilgrims' prayers in every language but English and after crossing the bridge there are arrows all over the place.

I arrive in Nájera with a terrible thirst and drink two icy cans of cola as Mini Clint comes steaming past, totally ignoring me, obviously on a mission from God. An idiot pilgrim stops just to tell me that drinking cola will only make me thirsty in the long run.

"Thanks for that!"

* * * *

Today my guidebook talks of yet another medieval miracle.

> Not far from here was the great battle of Claijvo (834), associated with the beginnings of the reconquest of Spain and the intervention of Saint James the Apostle, who appeared for the first time dressed as a Moor slayer. Here, Ramiro I of León defeated Abdurrahman II of Abdurrahman, and in the middle of the battle Saint James turned up on a big white horse and steamed into the Moors. He slew a thousand Moors to the right and two thousand Moors to the left. Then he returned safely to their homes "a hundred vestal virgins."

"Good-old Saint James!"

* * * *

Inside the pilgrims' hostel the hostelero looks perturbed at my passport and credentials, and relations are becoming strained.

"But where have you come from?" he asks quite angrily.

"Well, I was born in Dublin, but I live in England," I stupidly reply.

"No! Where have you come from today?"

His piercing eyes stare right into my soul. One wrong

answer here and I'm out on my arse. "Where the fuck have I come from today?"

Err . . . the clock is ticking, pressure building, what's the name of the fecking place!"

"Logroño!" shouts Yannik, overhearing my plight.

"Yes, yes, Logroño, Logroño, that's the place!"

The Spaniard shakes his head and stamps my credentials. As the doors open, I realize that I never had my passport stamped in Logroño due to the rude pilgrims' Boxing Day "sales-style rampage," and this is apparently what all the fuss is about.

Whilamena invites me for a beer along with a stout Dutchman called Theo. We find a nice quiet plaza in the middle of town, and Swiss John joins our group with an old Belgian pilgrim called Eric.

The Euro debate soon becomes heavily focused on how much weight we will lose throughout the journey as Theo clutches his well-fed midriff and laughs. If he wasn't a teacher in Holland, he could well have made a great bare-knuckles boxer, as he has the biggest hands I've ever seen and he's louder and more excitable than Swiss John. With my sparse knowledge of the Dutch language and the few English words that Theo knows, we get on like a house on fire.

"This is the second time I have gone to Saint James and I never lost any weight," moans Eric.

"Yes, but look at you! You have nothing to lose! He has nothing to lose. Look at him, nothing to lose!" says Swiss John back to our group, and our table erupts into fits of laughter as Eric shrugs and rolls a cigarette.

Later in a bar across from the hostel, the French biker and I watch the film *The Battle of Britain* dubbed in Spanish.

I'd been hoping the French biker would be a bit more like bikers I know back home, but alas, he has only two bottles of low-alcohol beer and then goes onto sparkling water, the lightweight!

Back outside the hostel I spend the rest of the evening with my new Dutch friends, with my mastery of the Dutch language improving slowly again. Theo has the loudest, most infectious laugh I have ever heard. I would also imagine he has the loudest snore to go with it, and as the night draws to a close I ask a very important question.

"What room are you in, Theo?"

# DOING THE FUNKY ROOSTER

MY PROPHESY HAS COME TRUE. In the distance, walking very slowly "like an Egyptian," is Cocker, with Belen, holding hands and canoodling like a pair of lovebirds.

"How're those boots of yours today? They do look very comfortable," I ask with a hint of sarcasm.

"Yeah, they're great," he lies. "It's just my ankles."

"No blisters then?"

"None at all." He grimaces.

"Seed exercises?"

"Speed exercises?"

Funnily enough, he's not in the mood for chitchat.

Ahead of them is the fabled couple with the donkey. An

English guy and a Dutch girl with a Spanish donkey that won't go up or down steps or over bridges.

I'm pleased I haven't got a donkey. Cocker is a bit of a donkey, I guess, and the way things are panning out between him and Belen . . . I reckon he could be hung like one, 'cause they're holding hands and staring madly into each other's eyes, giggling and joking. It could be said that it is indeed a miracle of the road.

Another miracle happened on this road, but a very long time ago when a German couple and their son called Hugo stayed here for the night in a local tavern. The innkeeper's beautiful daughter took a bit of a shine to the young German, but he gave her the el bow. So the naughty little minx slipped a silver cup into Hugo's bag, and as the family were leaving town they were chased down by angry locals. Poor-old Hugo was proclaimed guilty of theft and hung from a tree at the edge of town.

His parents on their return journey from Santiago heard their son's voice calling them and found him alive and well, still swinging from the tree with none other than Saint James himself holding him up.

Excitedly, they rushed to the local magistrate to inform him of the miracle. Looking up from his Sunday dinner, he said, "Your son is no more alive than these two roasted chickens on my plate."

The next thing, his dinner has sprouted feathers and starts doing the funky rooster all around his dining room. Needless to say, everybody lived happily ever after, including the hanged boy and the two birds.

The cock and hen were built a special cage in the church, and descendants of these birds can be seen now in the very same cage.

The legend goes that if you throw in a piece of bread and they eat it, you will arrive safely in Santiago. But if they don't eat it, you will die!

Cock and hen, more like cock and bull, if you ask me.

"Little donkey, little donkey on the dusty road, carry Mary, carry Mary safely on her way." Oh, for heaven's sake, now I'm stuck with that fecking song! Will I be driven insane by repetitive song syndrome? I'm beginning to wonder.

On arrival at Santo Domingo de la Calzada, I follow the arrows straight into the nunnery, to be greeted by none other than a nun in a glass booth. She checks my credentials and sends me upstairs to the pilgrims' quarters. From another room I hear beautiful singing and the place has yet again that air of sanctity about it, with bad pilgrim behavior at an all time low. Theo tells me there's a proper bath down the hall, so I wait hopefully by the door, listening to the splashing from within. After what seems an eternity, the door opens, followed by a waft of sweet-smelling steam and a lovely wet girl wrapped in a towel. She gives me a cheeky little smile as I watch her cute little arse go off in the direction of the pilgrim dormitory, and I recognize the cute little arse belonging to the girl near Puente la Reina. It seems that things are looking up at last, until I wipe the mirror and spot the big scabby sore on my lip.

"Bastards!" I swear, and a lightning bolt charges in the heavens. The powerful aura of female nakedness lingers in the steamy room, charging the atmosphere with passion and frustration. As sure as hell, all the hot water has gone, so I settle for a cold bath, extinguishing any ideas of a crafty trumpet polish, undoubtedly a top trump of religious misdemeanor.

Back in the room, Theo and Whilamena look like they are

planning a robbery. They whisper me over and we go through the plan. Immaculate Angel Benny from ABBA has let them in on a bit of a celestial secret. The nuns' canteen at the back of the building does cheap meals for worthy pilgrims—all for six euro and the flash of our pilgrim credentials. But woe betide we tell any of the rabble! A deal is a deal. With the coast clear, we sneak out the building and run straight into Manuel and Swiss John, both babbling on excitedly about some kind of mushroom festival in the town.

"Yeah, we're off for a look at the chickens in the church," I tell them.

"No, no, no, we've just been at the church," shrieks Swiss John.

"It's closed because of the fiesta," says Manuel, almost gleeful.

"Oh well, we better go and have a look at this fiesta instead."

We stride off quickly as he gets out his step machine and tells us his latest score.

* * * *

Like a trio of secret agents, we sneak around, watching out for sight and sound of rude, suspicious pilgrims. Unhindered, we get to the kitchens and part with six euro to a polite young nun. Thankfully we are the only pilgrims in this sea of black and white.

Good-old Benny, the angel. His wisdom is obviously sent from above. We dine on salad starter, chicken, chips, and free wine: the full monty of good-old pilgrim indulgence. Unfortunately, halfway through dinner Theo's loud and cheerful volume level peaks out at 130 decibels while he tries to describe in Dutch, with his arms flapping, what would happen if his meal suddenly grew feathers and flew off the table.

An elderly nun screws up her face and adjusts her hearing aid as a universal "Shush" echoes through the canteen.

Theo's big hand goes to his mouth, his eyes as wide as saucers, and for a split second, total silence as priests, nuns, and cooks breathe a big sigh of relief as calm is restored just in time for dessert. I reckon it's a good job we never brought Swiss John, with his high-pitched shrieking yes, yes, yesing, and Theo's booming voice at full blast in the same room surely a recipe for decibel disaster.

Fed and watered, we venture back out into the sun toward the town center, marveling at the colorful red and yellow banners flying from the windows and balconies. An equally colorful procession of Santo Dominican musicians passes through the busy streets, with their rosy red cheeks blowing hard into their cornets and bugles while others theatrically pour wine down their throats from strange horned drinking vessels. They look a lot like merry swashbuckling pirates, and people clap and yell as they pass. Somehow I find myself separated from my companions, and a mysterious lady pulls me by the arm into a large gray building, immediately thrusting a glass of wine into one hand and a big hunk of bread and cheese in the other. Things are definitely looking up!

I stand around for a while in the company of the well-dressed dignitaries and professional people, some of whom are again pouring wine into their mouths through these odd-looking bottles.

I nod and laugh with various people, about god knows what, and as soon as my glass is empty, people are falling over themselves to fill it up again. I quaff my wine and start to make for the door, but a rush of bodies swarm all over me, and before I know it, I have yet another large glass of red wine and two big crusty cobs with cheese to a chorus of more nodding and laughing. This time I gradually edge my way toward the door, and with a hearty gulp of my wine, and the bread in my jacket pockets, I escape unnoticed into the noisy plaza.

* * * *

Romeo and Juliet walk hand in hand in a dreamlike state. They see me coming and both go red. Cocker pulls his hand away from Belen and pretends to cough, shuffling nervously while Belen bites her nails. We wander around for a while and find a quiet bar for a few afternoon transfusions, then make our way across to the old pilgrims' hospital, which is now an expensive Parador. A plaque on the wall says that Saint Francis of Assisi once stayed here, and I turn to find Lord Cocker lounging around on the expensive furnishings like he owns the place.

A polite little man in a blue suit appears and asks us if we are guests.

"No," we reply.

He then politely asks us to leave. So we go to the church to see the magic chickens as I explain to them the legend of Santo Domingo.

"Right, this is how it goes: If the chicken eats your bread, you will arrive in Santiago, but if he doesn't, you will die! OK? I'll go first!"

I flick my bread through the bars of the coop, and it's gone in a flash.

Next at death-by-chicken knockout is Cocker, who stands back from the bars and throws like a drunken darts player. The cockerel gets it in his beak and shakes it straight back through the bars of the cage, and it ends up on the floor at our feet.

"That's you, fucked!" I laugh at Cocker's aghast expression.

Belen looks very worried. She crosses herself at the altar and begins to pray before it's her turn. Good idea, Belen!

"Dear God, sorry for just swearing in church and swearing in the nunnery earlier. Amen. Oh, and please help Cocker and Belen get to Santiago in one piece, please, if it's not too much to ask. Amen again."

Belen drops her bread into the cage. It lies there for almost an age until the hen bird grabs it and flicks it back out through the bars, and Belen begins to cry. Cocker to the rescue!

* * * *

Back out in the streets, the Santo Domingans feast from big cauldrons of mushrooms, and more blood of the pilgrim is spilled. I tell Cocker a great story about the last time I dined from a huge pot of strange mushrooms at a Dutch hippie festival.

An hour after eating them I still couldn't feel anything trippy in the head department, so I went back and complained, so the guy gave me a free second helping to make sure. Ten minutes later my world very suddenly became like the inside on a kaleidoscope, and then for some reason I believed myself to be Robin Hood of Sherwood Forest and gave away all my belongings, including my passport and wallet to a total stranger to look after for me. Then I took off all my clothes, folded them neatly, and climbed a large oak tree, where I remained for quite some time, deep in conversation with the leaf spirits, tree pixies, and bark monsters until the branch I was sitting on suddenly snapped, and I fell back to earth, badly grazing my bollocks on another branch that broke my fall. Luckily, I landed on top of a plastic table full of food and drink, which smashed into pieces, causing an abrupt end to a family picnic.

"They've never been the same since!" I tell him.

"Who, the picnickers?" asks Cocker.

"No my balls, man," I tell him, giving them a quick adjustment.

"Oh my goodness!" says Cocker, looking gravely concerned for my mental health. The story doesn't translate well for Belen, probably for the best, really. So I shut my big mouth and we take a steady walk back to our quarters.

# THE LAST SUPPER

THEO, SNORING LIKE A WOUNDED BUFFALO, has dislodged a couple of tiles from the roof of the nunnery, also dislodging a few more of my brain cells in the process. We leave Santo Domingo behind and continue down the strange road to Saint James. Our conversation this morning is one of Camino walking songs.

"Walk like an Egyptian!" shouts Cocker rather appropriately.

"Walking back to happiness—who ha oh yeah," I sing.

"This ain't no technological breakdown oh no, this is the road to hell."

"Chris Rea. I know that one," says Cocker.

"I'm on a highway to hell. AC/DC!" I love that song.

"Come on, Belen, sing us a song," we plead.

She acts all shy and coy and her pretty face goes crimson.

"Yeah, come on, sing us a song," Cocker pleads.

"Please, Belen."

She starts a little cautiously but then breaks into the most beautiful Spanish ballad I've ever heard and we clap our hands, delighted. It was worth all this pain just to hear her sing. Unfortunately, the game starts to take a turn for the worse with Cocker's version of "Walk This Way" by Aerosmith when farm dogs in a nearby yard begin to howl like wolves, thus signaling the end of our morning's entertainment.

Yet again our pace gets slower and slower, with Cocker staring at his antique watch, tying his laces every two minutes, and our jolly conversations having ceased. I get the message, though—two's company, three's a crowd!

I bid them a good day and hightail it down the hillside, coming to rest beside a deserted farmhouse. I roll down my knee support bandage and apply some deep heat relief cream to my ailing knee before rejoining the road.

I'm alone again, with no one in sight, and I'm busting for a leak.

A minute later I'm happy again, but alas only briefly, as a strange burning sensation in my shorts begins to gain momentum. At first I give it a rub and hope it goes away, but instead it gets worse and worse and worse. My penis feels like it's on fire, so I throw off my pack and whip down my shorts to investigate the unpleasant sensations. Now, in addition to administering deep heat relief cream to my injured knee, I have also managed to administer a smear of the phosphorus-like fire lotion directly on to my own bellend.

"AAAAGGGGHHHH!"

It burns like napalm, and no amount of water will wash it off. So I take my towel from my pack and rub the wet corner on the affected area while doing a war dance. With my shorts around my ankles, I'm rubbing frantically just as two gargoyle-faced crones come past.

*"Hola, buen . . ."* They stop midsentence with their mouths wide open. Caught red-handed! Or red-helmeted, as the case may be.

As more people come up behind me, I pull up my shorts and press on in agony, bringing back a painful childhood memory. My friend James Lewis told me that if you put aftershave on your willy it would make it bigger, and being twelve years old, I believed him.

I remember the pain and the smell of Hai Karate aftershave as I relive the moment on this Spanish hillside.

To take my mind off the pain, my repetitive song syndrome kicks in, and today's song is the ever-popular Trevor and Simon classic:

*"Old woman, old woman, are you fond of dancing?"*

*"Yes sir, yes sir, I am fond of dancing!"*

Over and over again the lines of that loopy song play like a broken record, and as the pain subsides in my shorts, I begin a series of violent sadistic fantasies about what I would do to someone I caught stealing my motorcycle. I arrive at the hostel in Belorado in a bad mood with a scuffed helmet.

\* \* \* \*

Today some bright spark has formulated an anti-stampede queuing system, and I'm told that I'm twenty-second in line by a highly obnoxious pilgrim. So I either stand in the queue and wait or I can leave my pack with a yellow Post-it note with number twenty-two stuck on it. "Fuck that!"

So I light a cigarette in the shade and drift into a murderous fantasy.

\* \* \* \*

An army truck pulls slowly into the square, reverses, and kills the engine. The pilgrims look across, getting excited while pushing, shoving, and cursing each other in the frenzy.

"Ya, at last, ze ostel owner comes to let us in and I am first!" shouts Dagmar, elbowing Christophe hard in the ribs.

"Last one inside is a nincompoop!" laughs Pierre.

"Women and children first!" shouts the round Irish lady.

"Fuck the women and children!" shouts the rude Frenchman.

"Have we got time for that?" says the fat Belgian, gleaming.

Two evil-looking soldiers climb out of the truck and walk casually around to the back. One of them smirks as the other flicks the butt of his cigarette and spits in the direction of the pilgrims as they drop the tailgate and throw back the heavy flaps.

Suddenly the pilgrims break rank, and the Irish lady is trampled in the pandemonium.

*Clunk! Click!*

Five long bursts of automatic fire spit venomously from the back of the truck, scything down the unruly rabble. For a second the plaza falls silent as the two soldiers pull out their luger pistols and stroll across to finish off the dying and wounded.

As fantasy returns back to reality, Dagmar is screaming, clutching her pack, frantic and fearful.

"I am not pushing in your silly queue; I am only reading what it says on the noticeboard, you stupid woman," says Swiss John, laughing in frustration. He sees me and walks across in amazement.

"I was only reading what it said on the noticeboard," he whines.

Across from the main hostel is an open door to one of the dormitories, and we decide to have a quick look in the room.

"I'm not staying here," says Swiss John, turning on his heel.

For the first time in my life, I see bunk beds three stories high, and I would put my life savings (if I had any!) on the fact that I would be allocated a top bunk, with bunkmates the fat Belgian and Dagmar.

"Let's get out of here!"

We hit the road expecting another few hours of painful walking, but just a block away we arrive at a quiet hostel with hardly a soul in sight. It's too good to be true. Our host is a very jovial chap called Javier, who proudly shows us around the spotless kitchen, washroom, and laundry room. Inside, the spacious dormitory has brand-new, modestly spaced two-story bunk beds made from solid pine. I have a lovely hot shower, and I even manage a nice little siesta without the need for earplugs.

We can't believe our luck. With all my clothes in the washing machine and Swiss John asleep, I venture back up the road. In a side street I even stumble across not one but two very dingy and dilapidated Irish theme bars, within spitting distance of each other and both . . . unfortunately closed. In the plaza I see Cocker wandering around like a pinball trying to read his Pablo Coolio and Belen wandering about with a cell phone stuck in her ear—probably the elderly boyfriend balancing on a barrel with a noose around his neck by the look on her face. Cocker sees me and strolls over. He's wearing a great big plant-pot-shaped hat with a seashell sewn on the front.

"What the fuck do you look like?" I ask him.

He sits down beside me and takes it off.

"Belen bought it for me, to say goodbye," he says sadly.

I'd totally forgotten he was leaving; tomorrow he's taking a bus down to Madrid to meet the Fockers. I mean Cockers.

I notice he has a lot of scratches all over his chest, and he lifts his T-shirt and shows me his stomach. Some of them are quite severe.

"I fell down a riverbank when we were having a picnic," he says.

"Rolling around with Belen more like," I jest. "What's wrong with her, anyway?" I ask him.

Cocker tells me that poor-old Belen is not actually on the phone to her elderly suicidal boyfriend as I suspected, but to her father back in Salamanca. Her brother who suffers from a learning disability had gone missing and has resurfaced in Magaluf. Belen has been given the task of bringing him home again safely, leaving me quietly disappointed, as I was secretly hoping to introduce one Bellend to the other at some point after Cocker's departure.

We arrange to meet later, and he goes back to support Belen. I watch as they walk off, arm in arm into the madhouse of a hostel. I can safely say they are, without a doubt, the oddest-looking couple I have ever seen in my life, even beating the other oddest couple I ever saw: Rastafarian gentleman and burka-clad Muslim lady I once spotted in a very dodgy part of Rotterdam one evening.

In his haste to console Belen, he has left his silly book on the stone step wrapped tightly in a large elastic band, so I pick it up and take it with me until I see him later.

On the way back to our pristine and erbert-free hostel, I spend fifty euros on different rash creams and painkillers, including white cotton gloves and a fifteen-euro lilac headscarf to protect my sun blistered neck and ears. I may look like a total pillock, but as long as I'm not itching, I'm not bothered. I report back to Swiss John and find my washing neatly folded on the bed as I take my time to apply the correct creams to the correct areas and manage yet another refreshing siesta.

That evening we meet up in the restaurant, and being hungry is an understatement, so I've cleverly managed to seat myself in between Cocker and Manuel in case there is any mix-up with vegetarian requirements or weight-loss issues. We are joined by the insanely jovial Swiss John, Theo, and Whilamena. Jan and Sarah sit across at another table, as does the kinky Dutch teacher and his student lover.

The donkey guy wanders in, looking a bit dusty, followed by Dagmar, Delacroix, Christophe, the nice Irish lady, and the rude Frenchman.

This being Cocker's last night for a while, I intend to give him a good-old sending off, as we've been through a lot in our short time together. So we start the evening with a couple of double brandies to celebrate, and everyone is having a really good time, but poor-old Cocker gets a bout of melancholia because he's missing Belen.

"Don't worry. I bet you'll see her again."

"I won't," he cries. "She's got back with her boyfriend."

"Oh, never mind, have some more wine," I tell him.

"Plenty more fish in the sea!" says Swiss John, laughing.

Poor Cocker, he makes up for it by drinking more and more, until halfway through our main course he slurs to a halt and almost slides off the table onto the floor. As I help him up, he gets all stroppy and argumentative, followed by happy, then sad, as emotion and alcohol take over. He laughs again about doing the Camino on a "pie." Then his eyes begin to close a little, and he announces that he wants to go back to the hostel.

"I need to fucking kip!" he slurs loudly.

Whilamena and Theo look puzzled at our inebriated friend. A *kip* in Dutch means *chicken*, opposed to English slang for *a kip*, which means *sleep*. I shrug and order a strong coffee for my friend in an attempt at sobering him up a bit, and he takes one of my cigarettes and balks.

"Bleurgh!" he yaks as the nicotine spins his drunken mind.

"Oh yeah, you only smoke those silk whatchamacallits?" I say.

"Cut!" he shouts angrily.

"What?" I feign deafness.

"Cut!" he shouts again, even angrier.

"Silk what again?" I ask, hammering another nail in his coffin.

"Silk fucking Cut!" He bangs his fist down on the table, knocking over an empty wine bottle and sending a spoon and napkin flying.

Unfortunately for Cocker, *kut* in Dutch means *cunt*, and the kinky underpants-wearing Dutch teacher stands and turns to Theo and says in English, "Kindly tell your friend to mind his filthy language!"

Then Theo and Whilamena have a heated discussion in Dutch with the disgruntled teacher about a chicken, a kut, and a ball-sack apparently! As 10:00 p.m. approaches, we leave the restaurant and bid a final farewell to our drunken friend. We hope to see him again as he hobbles out of sight, but never out of mind.

"Do you think . . . err, he and the girl, did they . . . ?" asks Swiss John, dismissing the notion with a shake of his head.

"No, I don't reckon so!" I tell him.

"And what was the matter with the Dutch people tonight?"

"I have no idea."

# SIGHT OF 114 MIRACLES, NEARLY 115

IT'S A FRESH MORNING, with not too many people around, and I fantasize about tearing up these tracks on a motocross bike.

"The Camino del dirt bike." That would be great, but considering the injuries I've sustained just on two feet, maybe not!

As I arrive in the medieval pilgrims' complex of San Juan de Ortega, I'm getting some very funny looks from fellow pilgrims, including the two old crones from yesterday. If it's not the alfresco wanking, it's definitely my latest fashion trend of looking like some kind of cross-dressing bedouin snooker referee, in my new lilac headscarf and white cotton gloves. Now that Cocker has gone, I'm definitely the worst-dressed pilgrim of all.

**＊ ＊ ＊ ＊**

San Juan de Ortega is a neat little place, starting with an old stone church as you enter the hamlet, followed by a small monastery in need of repair, then the pilgrims' hostel and a bar.

Salvation, sin, and siesta, all under the same roof.

Impatient pilgrims crowd around the entrance, looking at their watches, with their brain cells melting under the midday sun. Good-old Swiss John arrives and has a violent Mexican standoff with a huge safari-suited German. With his fat sausage-munching face wobbling like a jelly at poor-old Swiss John, who, yet again, is innocently trying to read the noticeboards at the hostel entrance. Due to the display of rudeness, Yannick wonders if he should go farther down the road, but he quickly thinks again because to the stifling heat and goes to fetch us some wine instead. I peel off my already-filthy gloves and scratch all my blisters until they bleed. Thankfully Yannick returns with wine, which I drink down in one.

**＊ ＊ ＊ ＊**

Inside the old stone bar, the Spanish workmen drink brandy and cackle away in a cloud of smoke as a group of American pilgrims dine on lovely-smelling pork chops and new potatoes. One of the Yanks sounds a lot like Ned Flanders from *The Simpsons*, and I listen in as he tells his equally monotone cronies about his exhausting bus and taxi journeys, due to twisting his ankle and getting a blister on his big toe.

"*Dos vino tinto, por favor,*" I say to the barman.

"Grand day," he replies as I point at the wine.

"Very warm out there, though," I tell him, and the day gets

grander as he fills two big glasses to the brim.

I've run out of cigarettes and the bar only sells the local brand called Ducados. They can't be too bad; everyone's smoking them.

Back outside in the picnic area we discuss our theories of whether or not Cocker and Belen committed the original sin. Although his back and stomach were covered in scratches, I'm still inclined to believe he fell down a riverbank, because I can't imagine him in throes of passion with the gorgeous Belen.

"I don't think we will see him again," says Swiss John sadly.

"The omens were not looking good, especially when the chicken threw his bread out of the cage. That's when I knew he was in trouble," I tell them.

Swiss John and Yannick look equally puzzled.

"The chickens at Santo Domingo—they threw his bread out the cage. That's when I knew he was fucked! He left me his book, though."

"What are you talking about?" says Swiss John.

"Oh, never mind. I need a cigarette."

At the first draw on the Ducados, I'm getting subtle aromas of horse shit, which burns my throat, making me reach for a large gulp of wine. The second hit has my palate experiencing the vague sensation of CS gas mixed with pepper spray, and the third and final hit—hints of burnt plastic and car tire as my head spins wildly.

"Ooh, Duca-fucking-dos," I cough and screw up my face.

Today might be a good day to quit smoking.

A stout Spanish lady arrives, rattling a bunch of keys, and it all kicks off around the entrance of the old building as more pilgrims arrive, including Theo, Wilhamena, Jan, and Sarah. Then the Italian yoga girl with a head injury, the rude Frenchmen, and, last but not least, the Dutch youths arrive to add to the chaos and volume.

A trio of bare-chested Dutch boys run screaming out of the church, followed by a loud piercing wail from within.

"Get out!" screams the demonic voice as the stout lady charges through the door. "And stay out, ye fecking orange heathens!" she shouts, violently waving a stiff brush. We all let out a cheer as the boys throw on their football shirts and skulk off into the dormitories with their tails between their legs.

"About time someone got topside of those noisy fuckers," I say.

Swiss John and Yannick agree.

After a few more glasses of wine I haul my weary body and heavy pack inside the building and have a cold but refreshing shower. It's too hot outside, so I venture back into the cool bar and try to write.

I can't believe I'm covered in these strange itchy blisters with a great big sore on my lip. My poor-old body is itching inside out, and my feet feel like I've done time in one of Saddam Hussein's torture clinics—the one's run by his two sons: Queer Say or Hear Say or whatever their names are. I read somewhere that they would skin a man's feet, then have a goat lick the wounds, pretty similar really to how my feet feel today! So to take my mind off things, I read a story from my guidebook.

San Juan de Ortega, whom this little village is named after, was a local man who founded a community of Augustinian monks who went on a massive building spree consisting of churches, hospitals, and paths for pilgrims. He was also good friends with funky roosting Saint Dominic, who built the church in Santo Domingo de la Calzada back down the road. San Juan is buried here in the church that he helped build.

I bet he even built this bar I'm in now. The best bit of the story is about a special carving showing the annunciation and the visitation of the Holy Ghost in Joseph's dream and Christ's nativity. That on each equinox, March 21 and September 22 at precisely 5:00 p.m. solar time, a single shaft of sunlight pervades the darkness of the church, creating the almost heavenly illusion that the Holy Ghost is illuminating the pregnant bump of the Virgin Mary. Wow!

I thought this place was special. So, I drink some more wine to celebrate and have a little look at this Pablo Coolio book Cocker left behind. As I flick the well-worn pages, I come to the seed exercise and read what those two plonkers were up to in Puente la Reina.

The seed exercise is like something we used to do in infant school, with our arms extending and our little fingertips reaching for the sun as we pretended pretending to be a tree, or was it a teapot or whatever the fuck it was anyway? All a bit silly, if you ask me.

A bit too much gangster tripping by the sounds of things, Mr. Coolio!

So I wrap it back up, hoping I do bump into Cocker again because he can gladly have it back. I've had enough of drinking wine, so I order a nice cool bottle of San Miguel and join the friendly faces back in the picnic area. In the space of half an hour we have a good little party in flow, with Theo bellowing out laughter, Jan and Sarah still laughing about Scunthorpe, and Swiss John lying in the grass, making strange noises and pulling equally strange faces, and I wonder yet again if he has X with him. Also joining the party are a cool German girl called Sonja and yoga girl Alyssa. Late in the afternoon the bar runs out of normal San Miguel, so we hit the export stuff, as well as loads more red wine. Add the old Ducados to that equation and we're all well on our way to oblivion.

I really wish we had a guitar, but after a fruitless search for the Brazilian Afro man, we make do with my harmonica and "Dirty Old Town" and then the traditional Irish song "The Wild Rover."

"No, nay, never," booms Theo. "No, nay, never no more," he sings, banging his massive fist down on the table and sending a minor tremor through our bodies.

Jan drunkenly manages an almost word-perfect "Tie Me Kangaroo Down, Sport" to great applause from the happy faces gathered around the table. But behind them I see authentic inquisition-faced pilgrims casting us the evil eye, no doubt fantasizing about an array of exotic genital torture devices and which one of us to pick first to try them out on. The equally medieval sight of man and donkey comes wandering into view, and the church bells toll for mass. We all fall silent for a moment to gather our drunken thoughts.

Aussie Jan has one eye open—she is proper pissed up, staggering around and slurring her words as we file quietly into the church and take a pew. I can't take my eyes off poor-old Jesus hung up there on the cross, and I feel like I want to make him a cup of tea for some reason. The service finally gets under way, and as per usual, most of us can't understand a word of the ceremony, just mumbling in the wrong places in a state of confusion. I look up at poor-old Jesus again and say sorry for being drunk in his presence, and when we kneel to pray I ask him if he can get me to Santiago in one piece. One of the carvings shows the sinners in hell, and the way things are going, it feels like I've got a one-way ticket. But saying that, where will all these so-called pilgrims like Dagmar, Christophe, and the fat German end up when they die? As I shut my eyes to pray, a vision of them all pushing, shoving, and quarreling at the pearly gates invades my drunken mind, and I figure that I'll stick with hell. Well, once I've done my purgatory first, of course.

As the ceremony ends, the priest leads us out a different set of doors into a beautiful old courtyard with ivy climbing through the cracks in the walls. I'm pleasantly surprised that all this was behind here, and Father Alonso explains that every penny from the hostel goes into restoring this place to its former glory. There's certainly a magical energy here, and even in my drunken state I can feel it's a very special place. Suddenly a moment of clarity hits me! This is what I should do at the end of the pilgrimage! I'll return here and help restore this building!

I see myself pottering around in the air of sanctity, repairing old doors and window frames and drinking wine in the bar with the Spanish workmen every dinnertime, giving foot massages to nice lady pilgrims every evening. This could be it.

"Saint Eduardo de Ortega. I like the sound of that." As soon as we finish this tour and I sober up a bit more, I'll find Father Alonso and tell him my vision. I'm sure he'll be thrilled to hear of my plans. I just know it!

The holy father leads us upstairs into a large room, and we sit at a long row of tables with Yannick at the end, silhouetted against the backdrop of a large window, through which the evening sun illuminates the trees. I feel calm, serene, and at peace with Yannick as a Scandinavian biker Jesus and we his

# BUTCH CASSIDY AND THE
# SPONGEPANTS KID

MY BED SHAKES VIOLENTLY as my bunkmate leaps down to the floor. Morning has broken, and I'm still heavy with wine. My tongue has stuck firmly to the roof of my mouth, and my soul is barren, laid waste, devoid of enthusiasm. I just want to curl up and die. As I loosen my tongue I taste red wine and garlic. The light comes on and with it more brain pain as the Euro babble reaches unprecedented levels. So I bury myself in my ripped sleeping bag the best way I can and wake a few hours later to total peace and quiet . . . and fear . . . Jesus! What was I up to last night? Pangs of Roman Catholic guilt rack my brain. What did I say to the priest?

Oh no! I hope I didn't volunteer for anything I shouldn't have!

It takes me an age to get going as the stout Spanish lady comes into the room with her mop and bucket. I frighten her as much as she does me and her look says it all . . . I need to leave!

It's 7:30 a.m and my head is still pounding. I know I did or said something to someone but I can't remember what.

Why do I drink so much? I curse myself.

I say goodbye to San Juan de Ortega and get back on track.

The gorgeous German girl is now walking toward me. I remember seeing her last night but avoided her due to my shabby appearance and even shabbier behavior, and now she is heading my way.

She smiles as she approaches, and I don't know where to look.

"Forgotten something?" I stupidly ask.

To which she replies telepathically, "No shit, Sherlock!"

I feel immediately foolish but manage to catch another glimpse of her tidy arse as my hands and whole body begin to itch like crazy.

Dark clouds gather across the stony mountainside and I catch up with Sonja and Alyssa.

Sonja laughs. "Hey, you were very drunk last night!"

"I know," I say, hoping for her to expand a little.

"Can you even remember?" laughs Alyssa.

"I remember talking to that donkey," I tell them.

"Do you remember pretending to be a seed with Swiss John?" Sonja laughs. "Oh, and wrestling with Hedrick?"

"Hedrick? Oh yes, good-old Hedrick!" I laugh, while wondering who on earth Hedrick might be!

I do hope it's not the name of the donkey.

**\* \* \* \***

I leave them behind to their girl talk as great big dirty blobs of rain hit my face and I begin the ascent into the hills of the Sierra de Atapuerca. In the thick black fog I first overtake one and then another horse-faced Dutch girl, who both look surprisingly like the Manchester United and Dutch international Ruud van Nistelrooy.

I feel an air of animosity between them, and I think they are not talking to each other for some reason. They look like they could do with some serious cheering up, but luckily for them I'm in no mood to take out my harmonica and entertain or rub some deep heat on my bobby's helmet and do a rain dance for them. As I deem by their faces that they are totally and hopelessly miserable, I decide to get away from them as quickly as possible, as they are putting my karma totally out of kilter with their sour and brooding energies.

At the top of the sierras, the mists close in and I feel like the last man standing. On my left is a rickety old barbed-wire fence and beyond it no-man's-land. A crack of lightning illuminates the sky, followed by a loud boom of thunder this time. It painfully rattles through my brain, and here I am a perfect conductor for a million volts of wrath. Now would be a good time for God to strike me down for all my past and present ill behaviors and religious misdemeanors.

But to put it in the immortal words of the great chief Sitting Bull:

"Today is not a good day to die!"

"Today is in fact a shit day to die!"

The rain lashes down even heavier as I head farther into the storm and I'm soaked to the bone. As the mists clear, I finally pick up the arrows on a tarmac road. Up ahead in the distance, one tall and one small person walk hand in hand. As I get closer I hear the voices of a woman and child. As I pass by, the mother says a staunch "Hello" and the little boy just smiles with his cheeky little SpongeBob SquarePants face, absolutely soaked to the bone, poor little fella. I wish I had some of those boiled sweets left. They might cheer him up a bit.

In the village of Orbaneja I dive out of the rain into a road-side bar for a warm-up and a coffee. Sitting at the table next to me is a strange German couple I haven't seen before. She looks very fresh, strong, and healthy. Amazonian almost, with a face that wouldn't look out of place in a Yankee sandwich on the front cover of a hard-core porn magazine. But her lover looks the total opposite. It looks to me as if she's wearing him out, the lucky bastard. It's not fair! She should be with someone like me. I could handle it. No problemo!

The doors opens and in walk mother and son. I quickly deduce from her age and his height that she must have had the little chappie quite early in life. She must be in her mid-twenties and the boy prepubescent. It happens! A boy I know back at home got his sixteen-year-old babysitter pregnant when he was just twelve, the dirty little fecker! But like I say, it happens.

The tiny boy takes off his wet jacket, and a very large and very wet pair of breasts flop out from under the wet T-shirt.

The poor-old Spanish barman almost eats his lit cigarette in shock, while Spongepants delves in her pack for a dry top.

All her stuff is wet through, so the little girl squeaks faintly to her friend, who has a massive hissy fit as she goes through her own pack to find a dry T-shirt for her wet little friend, which she thrusts angrily in her face. Poor Spongepants squeaks a faint thank you and heads for the bathroom, while grumpy bollocks sorts through her pack, sighing and moaning. Obviously she's the one who wears the strap-on (I mean trousers) in that relationship!

With all this commotion going on, I find myself staring at the large wall-mounted television, watching a disturbing daytime programme about ladies' incontinence problems, with a life-size model of the internal and external parts of a lady's anatomy on the screen above me.

"Nice program!" says Butch.

"Err, yeah!" I nervously agree.

Her little friend comes back from the toilet with a dry top on, and her nipples almost knock my hat off. I don't know where to look—fannies and bumholes, on the telly, little boy's tits, or the porn star sitting canoodling behind me!

The Lord definitely moves in mysterious ways—either that or he has a wicked sense of humor. The seven-foot German naturist at Roncesvalles, with a big loud mouth and an acorn-sized excuse for a cock; now a dwarflike girl with 34GG breasts and her bossy lesbian lover; and finally a dominant, sexually athletic female with a sickly weak male! I finish my coffee staring at the television as a lady's intimate parts are being tapped with a stick by a mad-looking professor and I think it's time to leave.

"Butch and Spongepants," I christen the lesbian lovers.

The cold rain brings me back to my senses, but I can't stop thinking about the two girls and what they get up to in their fully equipped lesbian dungeon. My fantasy comes to an end as a group of cackling French biddies overtake me quickly and the beautiful countryside making way for the dirty and industrial.

Cars and lorries scream along the motorway and the air

becomes foul with the fumes and the smells of the big city. Maybe I ought to get myself a room for the night with some fine wines and Belgian chocolates. I'll invite Butch and Spongepants for a bit of lesbian entertainment. But I catch a glimpse of my reflection in the glass of a shop window. "Maybe not!" I look like a homeless crack fiend. Toxic sweat oozes from my pores, leaving huge salty marks all over my ripped shirt, with scabs and sores on my ears, lips, and face. My hands have been itching so badly that I've scratched every tiny blister red raw and my face says *I need a fix!*

At a busy junction the arrows have completely vanished off the face of the earth. So again, I follow my instincts and signs for the cathedral. My hangover is really starting to kick in badly now and I'm getting more and more stressed out. So I light up a Ducados to help me think. After two hits the whole pack goes in the bin, closely followed by the carefully extinguished offender, and now I feel like shit.

Luckily I spot the German couple from the café studying a map, but suddenly they dart off and I give chase. They are a hard act to follow. Eventually, after chasing them for about a half mile and losing them a couple of times, they finally stop and get out their map. "The pilgrims' hostel?" I ask them in hopeful expectation, but they both shrug and shake their heads.

"No, it's not on our map," says the sickly man. "No, we are looking for the Crown Plaza Hotel," says the sex kitten, almost purring with delight. The lovers shrug and walk off, leaving me standing on the busy city corner.

"Thanks a million!" I curse. I bet they even made arrangements with Butch and Spongepants to join them in their suite for some debauched sexual antics. I scratch and bleed some more in utter frustration while I curse the yellow arrow man, yet again!

"It's all your fucking fault, you bastard!" I shout at the sky. Probably the exact words I would say to him before tipping the yellow paint over his head, then hitting him repeatedly with the tin.

Eventually a flurry of yellow arrows rain down on me and I find myself in the outskirts of the city, lost and confused. A kindly Japanese pilgrim coming the other way directs me to the hostel.

"*Rápido,*" he says. "The beds are running out."

I step up a gear and come to what can only be described as a jerry-built pilgrims' hostel, looking like the set of *The Great Escape* meets *Auf Wiedersehen, Pet*!

All we need now is a machine-gun tower, a pallet of bricks, and Jimmy Nail in his baggy underpants, stamping our credentials while swigging from a bottle of Beck's lager.

# CRINT EASTROOD

BURGOS MAY BE A GREAT PLACE to spend the weekend with your lesbian lover, but I need to get out of here, quick-style! The walk out of the city is, thankfully, much nicer than the one coming in, and I'm pleased to report that there are yellow arrows all over the fecking place.

I meet a speedy English pensioner called Mike. He's originally from Yorkshire. We have a lot in common. He tells me that this is the second time he has walked the Camino, his first attempt sadly ending in total hospitalization.

"Tendonitis," says Mike. "This time I'm taking it steady."

"Could have fooled me," I attempt to say, while inhaling part of my sandwich. For a moment everything stops; my eyes bulge as my lungs gasp for air, and on the third cough I propel the foreign object into the atmosphere and make another mental note never to eat and drink while running! I look up but Mike has gone. I watch as he tears off into the distance in a cloud of dust like the mighty Road Runner.

"Meep, meep!"

Farther down the road I take a leisurely lunch break in Rabé de las Calzadas.

The little café owner looks a lot like Kevin Moynihan, the hardworking, hard-drinking, tough Irish foreman I had in Holland during the nineties. Except that this guy is a third of his size but has the same head, piercing eyes and Thomas Magnum–style mustache.

*"Un jamón queso bocadillo, por favor,"* I say.

Little Kevin babbles away . . . something about a rock or a stone. He comes back from the kitchen with a stick of bread, then proceeds to beat the life out of it on the oak bar. Like a fool I tell him it will be fine, so he stands it on top of the coffee machine to breathe a bit of life back into it and offers me a Ducados while I wait. After five minutes or so he gives the bread another good doink on the corner of the coffee machine and shrugs once again.

Suddenly a crazed English lady makes a dramatic entrance by crashing through the doors in a fluster and panting at little Kevin.

"I need foooood!" she says in English, putting her finger in her mouth and acting like some kind of cavewoman.

"No," says little Kevin, "there's no bread left until I go shopping."

She understands the "No" bit but sees my resurrecting bread on the coffee machine and cries, "I haven't eaten for two days!"

Kevin says truthfully that there is no bread and that's that, but she thinks he's being awkward and starts to cause a scene. So little Kevin offers her a Ducados in an attempt to restore the peace. But she shrieks and sighs and then turns on her heel, throwing back her head, and says, "I suppose I'll just have to starve then!"

She wails again and flees in the same dramatic fashion. We both laugh as Kevin gives my bread a final crack on the counter, then takes it through to the kitchen, returning minutes later with what looks like a delicious sandwich full of chorizo, cheese, and tomato.

I open my mouth as wide as it will go and bite down hard, almost breaking off my two front teeth in the process. To prevent teeth damage, I put the sandwich on the bar and give it a good hard punch. Then, however painfully, I eat the lot, while being heavily scrutinized by little Kevin.

When I finish, he shakes my hand, gives me a free coffee, and awards me another Ducados—and, finally, a *"¡Buen camino!"*

* * * *

Back out on the strange road ahead in the distance, I see the remarkable sight of an enormous black lady making very awkward progress.

*"¡Hola, buen camino!"* she shouts in a jolly French accent as I give her a wide berth. As I pass through Hornillos del Camino, a strange man runs out of his house and starts shouting in my face, giving me quite a startle. The words "Fuck off, caveman!" roll off my tongue without thinking, and I walk off very proud of that one.

\* \* \* \*

In Hontanas I'm joined by the Japanese pilgrim I saw yesterday, and it turns out that he's actually Korean. He can't speak English and I can't speak Korean, but between us, we manage to have a bit of Eurocraic. He mimics the actions of a Wild West gunfighter, throwing back an imaginary poncho and firing at an unseen attacker. He blows the smoke from the end of his imaginary pistol and spins it on one finger before he reholsters and sits down, whistling a bit of Sergio Leone.

"Crint Eastrood," he says. "You like?"

"Clint Eastwood! Yeah, man!"

I'm beginning to get his vibe. I suppose these streets do look a little like those in the spaghetti westerns.

"Eddie." I introduce myself.

"Wee," he says.

"Nice to meet you, Wee." I shake his hand.

"No! Ree!" he says.

"Ah, OK, sorry, Ree."

"No, Ree!" he says excitedly, thrusting his pilgrim's credentials in my face. Lee Chatchapingyas is his name.

"Ah, Lee," I say, and a big smile plays out on his face. Meanwhile, the unmistakable figures of Butch and Spongepants appear on the horizon.

"Oh!" says Lee, as only Asians can, putting his hand close to the floor as if to measure a small person as we watch them approaching.

Lee's eyes almost pop out of his head as Spongepants's unmanageable puppies jostle in and out of her vest top. She struggles to take off her oversize pack as Butch tells her where to sit and what to do. Little Spongepants squeaks back like a church mouse, doing everything she says, and I wonder if it's about time that the tables were turned and Spongepants got to wear the strap-on for a change.

In Hontanas there are only so many imaginary gunfight and lesbian fantasies one can have, and clean, crisp, and clinical boredom has set in for the day. Luckily, Cocker's book provides the afternoon's entertainment as I tear small strips from the cardboard cover and fire them from the elastic band.

# L♥VE IS IN THE AIR

WE SET OFF FROM HONTANAS, gunfighting our way out of town, acting like a pair of clowns, much to the disapproval of some very authentic medieval faces, and we arrive in Castrojeriz quite early.

Lee decides he will go farther, but I fancy an easy one today. So I bid farewell to my Wild West Korean buddy and we have our final gunfight in front of the pilgrims' hostel. Lee shoots first and I fall to my knees, clutching my stomach as he blows the smoke from the barrel of his six guns. I watch him disappear into the distance, whistling the theme tune to *The Good the Bad and the Ugly*.

Speaking of which, an ill-mannered rabble begin to line up behind me tutting, sighing, and squabbling. Today I'm numero uno in the queue, and I shall guard my place to the very last drop of blood of the pilgrim. We enter the hostel in an orderly fashion and I'm first in the shower too, but the hot water on my hands inflames them more and I can't resist another frantic scratch until the water turns crimson.

The midday heat has evaporated any ideas of chemists into thin air. Luckily, I come across an Irish bar, and I'm its first customer of the day. I'm equally delighted when the barman pours my pint of Guinness the proper Irish way, joined by a plate of tapas. This is the life!

It's a great little bar for a knees up, but where is everybody today? There's not a soul in sight. I tire quickly of my own company and venture back to the hostel for a much-needed siesta. Unfortunately, I find my bed space invaded by a group of goofy-looking young Germans with their arms and legs hanging all over the place.

I gesture to my bed and they all look at me like I'm some kind of turd left by a Martian. When I wake up, they are still there, goofing, lolling about, and doing my head in. So I go back to the bar and read from my guidebook about Saint Anthony's fire—a highly contagious skin disease producing burning red blisters, which scourged Europe in the tenth and eleventh centuries. It's now seemingly making a comeback, starting with me as its first modern-day victim. Again I tire quickly of the Irish bar and head for the Spanish bar opposite the hostel. Inside the bar, workmen watch the bullfighting on a large wall-mounted television.

I can't help but watch as the opening ceremony commences with jeering crowds and crazy trumpet music.

The matadors enter the dusty arena, three abreast in their glittering suits like a trio of ballroom dancers. As the bull comes galloping into the arena, I let out a cheer, which doesn't go down too well with the bar-side spectators. I wonder if the bull is one of the legendary Miura bulls, the breed known as the "bulls of death" because they realize a bit quicker than ordinary bulls that the enemy is not the heart-shaped red cloth attached to the baton—it's the silly man in ladies' underwear holding it! The matador gets the better of the poor-old bull, and I can't watch as the dagger is drawn. I gaze out the window at the equally depressing sight of a load of boring erberts reading their Pablo Coolio and Shirley MacLaine novels, and yet again I wonder to myself for the umpteenth time why am I doing this pilgrimage thing, what good it's gonna do me and what I'm going to do afterward.

But hope springs eternal as a vision of beauty in the form of the German girl walks out of the hostel and sits down on the stone wall to read.

"Come on, Elvis, it's now or never!" I say to myself as I nip in the toilets to check my appearance and then casually walk out of the bar.

"Oh. *¡Hola!*" she says.

"*Hola*, I'm Eddie."

"Eva," she says. "Pleased to meet you," she adds with a smile.

We sit together on the wall and exchange pleasantries. Eva tells me that she's from Leipzig. She is a massage therapist and is also quite thirsty. So I invite her for a beer back across the road. One thing we have got in common is our love for animals, and we both cheer the unlucky bulls to the dirty looks of the dirty men.

A small man walks into the bar with a couple of shopping bags as I go up to get a refill, and his little face lights up. It's miniature Kevin Moynihan, the concrete bread man! He shakes my hand, delighted to see me, and buys me a Johnnie Walker whisky. No ifs or buts. It's mandatory!

I stand there with him like a spare part, nodding for five minutes while he tells his cronies about the kryptonite sandwich, even reenacting the part where I punched it and ate it. His friends are in stitches and we toast to "rockadillos" as I shake all their hands and eventually sit back down with laughing Eva. She thinks it's hilarious as miniature Kevin keeps looking over every ten seconds, raising his eyebrows, and fingering the corners of his moustache. Eventually he leaves, giving me the thumbs-up and a crafty wink before wishing me a *"Buen camino."* What a character! Eva is laughing again and I would love to keep her laughing all night long.

# SAINT ELMO'S FIRE; MAN IN MOTION

ALL ALONE ON THE STRANGE ROAD and not a soul in sight. Erbert-free, just the way I like it, really. I can't stop thinking about sexy Eva and her strong, shapely, well-made German legs. I like the way she talks, too, with her eyes wide and innocent like a baby deer's. But she laughs with a devilish twang to her sexy accent and I can quite easily imagine her naked with . . .

Suddenly something in the grass moves! At first I dismiss it as a mouse or snake and return to Eva, now stark bollock, except for a pair of jackboots, a riding crop, and a wicked grin!

The grass shakes me to my senses again and I carefully part the long strands. There before me is a small blue-and-white songbird with a blade of grass wrapped round his tiny leg, trapped and frightened.

So I very carefully unwrap his bonds and gather him up in

my hands, and he flies away to freedom. I feel fantastic all of a sudden. I've saved a little life and it's made my day.

They say a lot of famous people have walked the Camino. Saint Francis was one of them, and he would have been proud of my actions today. Anthony Quinn, the actor, walked the Camino, as did actress Shirley MacLaine, and the Scottish pop group the Proclaimers wrote a song about it called "500 Miles." I also heard tell that criminals were made to walk the Camino, carrying the body of their victim strapped to their backs as a medieval measure to prevent the murder of fat bishops.

I heard it said by a stout Englishman that the Devil will try to trick you three times while on the Camino.

It feels like he tricks me every day.

It's a pleasant and peaceful morning walking beside the old canal. I take out my harmonica and play the classic song "Dirty Old Town," an all-time Irish classic made popular by the Dubliners and the Pogues.

> *I met my love by the gas works wall*
> *Dreamed a dream, by the old canal.*
> *I kissed a girl by the factory wall*
> *Dirty old town, dirty old town.*

After a good-old bout of harmonica, I rest awhile beside the lock on the edge of town and read another story from my guidebook.

Frómista is the home town of San Telmo, or in English Saint Elmo, the patron saint of sailors and famous for Saint Elmo's fire. I wonder what kind of torment that was. Hopefully, not one to add to my own growing list of afflictions. "St. Elmo's

Fire" was also an eighties pop song by mulleted fop John Parr, as I seem to remember. My olden days pilgrim buddy Aymeric says this about Frómista:

> It is a land full of treasure, of gold and silver, rich in wool and strong horses and abounding in bread, wine, meat, fish, milk and honey. However there are few trees and the place is full of evil, bad men.

So, with Aymeric's words fresh in my head, I book into the modern hostel on the lookout for evil, bad men. Tucker arrives.

"What's up, dude? How's your bellend?" He laughs

"Jesus, Tucker, I thought you'd be in Santiago by now."

Tucker explains that for three nights he never got a wink of sleep due to people snoring, so he bit the bullet and stayed in a quiet pension and slept from 7:00 p.m. to lunchtime the next day. It's good to see him again, and he wants to know about Cocker and Belen. Did they or didn't they commit the original sin? Even Tucker agrees, it's highly unlikely Cocker got anywhere near her bodily treasures.

I invite him for a beer and we head into town to find a very seedy-looking bar, full of the unworked, unwashed, and probably direct descendants of those bad and evil men from Aymeric's days. They sit noisily playing cards and dominoes while smoking Ducados and small cigars with glasses of brandy or red wine. Even the barman looks like a dirty Mexican bandit, with sweat gleaming on his dark skin with a glint in his eye. All he needs is a sombrero and a few belts of ammo strapped around him and we're there. Due to the substandard hygiene of the establishment, we opt for bottled lagers and stare at the television screen. The Spanish news is in full swing with images of war-torn Iraq and al-Qaeda video footage of roadside bombs blowing up US Humvees. Bloodied children lie uncared for in filthy hospitals while greasy-looking politicians happily lie to us about the numbers of civilian casualties.

"God damn! Look at these guys!" says my American friend.

Now sinister bearded men spit venomous words to crowds of hate-filled people, burning flags, chanting and wanting to chop off our infidel heads.

"Dude, those guys should be nuked," says my Yankee pal.

"I met a hate-filled preacher once," I tell Tucker, and begin my story.

A week after al-Qaeda brought down the Twin Towers, my short-fused friend Gilbert and I and his long-suffering hippie girlfriend, Danni, were sitting on the terrace of the Engels bar at Rotterdam's Central Station, waiting for some money to arrive via wire transfer. Gilbert was foul, and to add to his mood, Danni was hassling him about all the money he owed everyone, how much he was spending on drugs and alcohol, and how much she was taking off him each week to pay the bills.

Now, why a hate-filled preacher should choose to stand next to our table and chant to the bemused citizens of Rotterdam is quite beyond me.

"Death to all infidels!" he shouts and screams.

Gilbert's eyes roll back in his head, and I feel a pressure shift in the earth's atmosphere. In one ear, Danni twists his melon about cocaine and violence, and in the other ear, hate-filled Harry and holy war.

Gilbert takes a deep breath, and Danni knows what's coming, so she wraps her body around his arm in an attempt to stop the bloodshed.

"Please, Gilly, no!" she screams.

"Fuck off, woman!" he shouts, easily shaking her free.

Danni wails and sobs into the table as Gilbert stands before the hate-filled cleric, face-to-face, nose-to-nose. This doesn't stop the radical ranting as Gilbert smirks menacingly. He wrenches the book out of his hate-filled hand and follows it up with an equally hate-filled, high-velocity Mancunian punch, making bone-crushing contact with the radical preacher's features. The erbert hits the pavement with a sickening thud as Danni wails louder into the table, crying the old chestnut, "Why does he have to be like this?" and I think to myself, *If I had a euro for every time I heard that this year, I'd have a private jet on twenty-four-hour standby at Schiphol airport.*

Gilbert turns to sit down but notices he's still holding the book. So in a grand finale, he throws the book into the air and boots it in a perfect arc onto the roof of Rotterdam's Central Station to a small round of applause from a few good citizens.

Gilbert sits back down at the table with his eyes twinkling, delighted with himself. However, a five-strong troop of heavily built, heavily tattooed Feyenoord skinheads enter the terrace heading straight for us! "Oh fuck!" My arse cheeks nip tight and my heart rate doubles as they swarm over our table, but instead of kicks and punches, it's smiles and laughter as they congratulate the unlikely hero, kissing his bald head and shaking our hands—all except Danni, who looks up for a split second, then throws her head back into her arms in a flood of tears.

"Yeehar!" shouts Tucker.

I shall have to give Gilbert a ring at some point and see if he's still alive.

# THE LAST POST

THE MORNING STROLL OUT OF FRÓMISTA begins with good omens and I'm making great progress, so I sit for a while beside the river and read a little.

> A thousand years ago this area was controlled by the Moors and on every market day the region had to supply 100 virgins to replenish their Harems. This all ended with the battle of Clavijo. When St. James appeared on a big white charger dressed as a pilgrim and slew 40,000 Moors.

"Jesus, it's no wonder they call him the Moor slayer!"
The American Ned Flanders sound-a-like approaches with his baseball cap on back to front, looking like some kind of idiotic hip-hop DJ with his two expressionless cronies either side,

creating a double misery effect of their presence.

"Everything OK, brother?" shouts Flanders.

"Yes, thank you!"

"Hey!" he shouts. "Hey!" Now he's standing right next to me.

I eventually look up from my book.

"Yes? Can I help you?"

"Hey, buddy, are you from the Confraternity of Saint James?"

"No!" I say sharply, praying he will go away.

"Okily dokily, brother, just thought I'd ask."

"*Buen camino,*" they all say together.

"God loves you, pilgrim!" shouts Flanders.

"He's got a funny way of showing it!" I shout back.

Confraternity of Saint James! Sounds a bit dodgy to me.

**\* \* \* \***

It's too early to stop in Carrión de los Condes, so I pass straight through and manage to dodge the unfortunate trio who I spot loitering around a lovely old monastery. It's another windless scorcher of a day as my feet drag up the dusty track, and the only thing keeping me going is a barrage of lines from more crazy songs:

*Catch me if you can, me name is Dan, sure I'm your man.*
*And I'm off to Lisdoonvarna at the end of the year.*
*I'm off for the bit of cráic, the women and the beer.*
*I'm awful shifty for a man of fifty.*
*Catch me if you can, me name is Dan, sure I'm yer man.*

The Brendan Shine classic keeps playing around my head like a stuck record, reminding me of a fella called Big Dan who drank in Tom Kiely's bar in Trim, where my father came from. Big Dan used to go AWOL from his isolated farm and go on the beer for weeks and weeks at a time, and that song would be playing on the jukebox constantly.

There's nothing to see for miles around, and I begin to fear I might have gone totally the wrong way, as I haven't seen an arrow since I got on this track. I seem to be passing the same poppy over and over again. For hours time stands still in this air-less vacuum, and over every small brow I long to see the familiar sight of a church spire, but each time nothing, endless nothing. I try to focus through the shimmering heat and begin to limp as a new addition to my never-ending set of problems begins to rear its ugly head directly in the heel of my left boot. I slowly enter the strange village of Calzadilla de la Cueza and find the pilgrims' hostel. Many pilgrims lay bedridden with bandages on their heads, shoulders, knees, and toes, lying exhausted and motionless in the heat. Flies crawl all over my face and hands, driving me totally insane. I quickly check in and seek the blood of the pilgrim immediately.

In the nearby hotel I meet Günter, a German pilgrim and soft-metal enthusiast with monotone voice and lank, greasy hair. His boring conversation slowly drains me of positive energy like an emptying bath, making me feel almost suicidal. Günter is also bandaged up to the eyeballs, and he tells me he fell down a rocky hillside. *Or was he pushed,* I wonder? Thankfully he's staying at the plush hotel and not the asylum, or I'd have slept in one of the caves just to get away from him. Yet again another Jonah to steer clear of.

It's still light when I get back to the invalids' ward, and now the world's most sunburnt German has arrived on the scene. Concerned pilgrims chase him around the room like a scene from Benny Hill with bottles of sun cream and after-sun as his skin peels off his face like grated cheese, all over the collars of his jacket, his beard, and his mustache.

But being the kind of man who would probably refuse to call the fire brigade if his house were burning down, I watch in disbelief as the sunburnt martyr rudely refuses all help, then lies down defiantly, fully clothed, hugging his pack and staring that thousand-yard pilgrim stare.

"What a douche nozzle"

## ACHTUNG! HEIL SHITLER!

AS THE LIGHTS GO on, the German is up and out the door like a rocket and I'm not far behind him.

*"Hola, buen camino,"* I hear from the road.

I look up as two cyclists zoom past, waving not at me but at the sunburnt German, who's crouched in the oilseed rape with his trousers around his ankles. His right arm is extended in classic Nazi salute, and he shouts *"¡Buen camino!"* while flourishing a piece of toilet paper at the two cyclists, who, to make matters worse, continue happily waving back at him!

*ACHTUNG! HEIL SHITLER!*

On a desolate track with a million croaking frogs all around, I stop at a memorial for yet another German man whose pilgrimage ended right here. I guess a lot of people never make it to Santiago, for one reason or another. With that in mind I sit eating my bocadillo at the side of the field, not noticing at first a dangerous, rabid-looking dog with demonic yellow eyes sitting at the side of the path.

He bares his horrible teeth and growls without sound. He looks frighteningly ill, so I throw him some bread and chorizo, but he just looks straight into my eyes, unmoving, unblinking.

I finish my sandwich slowly and carefully while hypnotized by the hell-bound yellow eyes of the devil dog. Then I back away from him a safe distance and hit the road. After a few hundred meters I look back, but he's thankfully nowhere to be seen. The sun has got his hat on again, and I arrive dazed and confused in the town of El Burgo Ranero.

**\* \* \* \***

The supposedly helpful picture in the hostel toilet is the funniest thing I've seen so far since Cocker's sandals. It's been altered slightly by a naughty pilgrim with a very childish sense of humor. Ten out of ten.

In the guestbook I see that none other than Cocker stayed here two nights ago. I wonder if I can catch up to him. . . but then again with my new injury, I'm not sure.

Back in the bedroom I gradually work up enough courage to operate on my painful heel. First, I sterilize my knife with my lighter, then wipe away the soot and prepare for the first incision. I take a deep breath and start cutting through layers of hard skin to get to the source of the pain. Eventually a mixture of agony and ecstasy floods from my heel, and I tidy the area, cutting away the dead flesh and plugging the hole with iodine-soaked gauze to prevent infection. Now all I need is the blood of the pilgrim for express pain relief and I'm all set.

Alyssa turns up, saying she's seen Eva earlier today and more than likely she will be staying here this evening. Three jolly Brazilian guys arrive with whom I'm sharing a room. One of them is wearing a "Jesus Saves" T-shirt, with Jesus's compassionate face on the front. I have a similar T-shirt but with a comedy goal-keeping Jesus diving through the air to catch a football. I put it on after my shower and we take some photos outside the hostel. They are a friendly bunch of guys, and I nickname them "the Three Amigos."

Their names are Ze, who speaks very good English; Rodrigo, who speaks a little English; and Ricardo, with not many words.

Ze tells us that he and Ricardo are teachers and Rodrigo is a medic.

It is the second time they are walking the Camino together.

At mealtime, the amigos and I throw all our food together and soon have a meal fit for a German queen, with salads, pasta, cheeses, ham, and fresh bread from the bakery. As I open the first bottle of wine, Eva arrives and I invite her and Alyssa to join us for dinner.

Our joviality around the table causes concern from the hostelero, who warns us all not to get drunk.

After dinner Alyssa goes onto the grass for a bit of yoga, giving me food for thought for some exiting new sexual positions, should I ever be lucky enough to find a flexible girlfriend. Eva appears, wearing tight blue velour shorts and a skimpy bikini top.

We end the night in the bar across the road for a few well needed beers

The barman can't take his eyes off Eva and neither can I, for that matter. She looks great, all tanned and healthy, and I love it when she laughs her naughty laugh. It really turns me on. I tell her about the little bird tied up with grass, and she tells me a similar story about frightening a cat, whose mouth opened in shock, releasing a little bird. "So we have both saved a little soul." She laughs, putting her hand on mine.

EL BURGO RANERO TO MANSILLA DE

LAS MULAS

## BUENAS NOCHES, SENORITA

MY FIRST IMAGE THIS MORNING upon opening my eyes is the bare bottom of an old lady from the bunk above me. Wildly balancing on one leg while pulling on a large pair of pants, she makes me feel strangely aroused, as I imagine that she would have been quite a looker in her days.

I arrive in Mansilla de las Mulas just before lunchtime and immediately get lost at an important junction. I once again follow my nose and eventually spot the usual bunch of misérables and a few friendly faces waiting outside the hostel. As luck would have it, there's a really good bar directly across the road, so I grab a quick beer to pass the time. Theo, Eric, and Swiss John reappear, as do the rude Frenchmen and English Mike, the Road Runner. They all join me happily at the table for wine and beer. The French guys don't seem too bad after all, as they get stuck into pints and large glasses of wine. One of them shows me his pilgrim's credentials with stamps all the way back from Le Puy in the garden of France. Viking Yannick arrives with a beer, and we all toast to our future and to the start of a great afternoon. After a couple of wines, I find I'm becoming more multilingual, remembering things in French I learned at school.

I laugh and joke with Theo, using the Dutch I picked up in Holland.

By the time Eva gets here, I will be speaking fluent German at this rate. Our group waits for the misérables to get inside, and then, one by one, they finish their drinks and check in.

I have a peaceful, easy feeling going on, and sure enough, playing in the background is that very song by the Eagles, so I wait until it's finished and go and check in myself

The hostel doesn't look much from the street, but once I'm inside it turns into a large courtyard with a balcony and a beautiful tree growing in the middle. There are loads of hanging baskets and potted plants hung all over the walls, and it is obvious that someone takes a great pride in this place. The hostel has a really positive feel to it. After a nice lukewarm shower, I feel like a new man. I get a top bunk in a nice clean upstairs room, and the newly arrived Three Amigos invite me for dinner. So I buy wine and mineral water for the meal and chance upon another little bar near the shop to enjoy tapas and vino served by a busty maiden, just like in the olden days.

Back in the foyer I meet an Austrian doctor by the name of Andreas and his good wife, Greta, who are talking about visiting a tenth-century church and would I, "Eduardo," like to join them. There is space in the taxi for a few more, if I know of anyone else who'd like to go.

I can't believe my luck.

Ten minutes later we are heading away from Mansilla in a big taxi with Dr. Andreas and Greta, Swiss John, and the Three Amigos.

The taxi driver and the amigos understand each other pretty well, so I ask about the large dinosaur nests that I've seen.

The taxi driver says they are storks' nests; some can weigh up to three hundred kilograms and have often been known to topple off buildings, crushing cars and often people.

After a short journey we arrive at the Church of San Miguel de Escalada, built by a community of monks in the early tenth century.

They certainly picked a very beautiful spot for it, and you can almost feel the magic in the air. This beautiful church had been built with a very Moorish influence, with fabulous porticos and smooth stone arches. Inside the church it's quite cool and peaceful, with fantastic marble pillars and a minimal old stone altar. Swiss John is like a child in a sweet shop, hugging each one of the marble pillars and telling me each one is giving off a different kind of positive energy.

"Yes, yes, yes," he keeps saying and nodding. "I can feel it. Can you feel it?" he asks us all merrily.

I have to agree this is the best church I've ever been in. No fancy altars or retable with spooky statues all over the place. Poor-old Jesus on the cross is nowhere to be seen. The place is filled with a universal peace.

Back at the hostel, Dr. Andreas won't take our money or our offer of food. He declines politely and decides on taking his lovely wife to a nice restaurant in the town, and we wish them well. In the kitchen, the amigos prepare the evening meal, and Swiss John loiters loudly as Eva and Alyssa arrive with even more bags of fine food. The large black girl Chantel comes into the kitchen, looking for Rodrigo.

She's heard he's a medic and is asking for inflammation relief. Fair play to Rodrigo, he gets his medic kit out and does the business as she drops her leggings on one side to reveal an arse cheek the size of Luxembourg. Ricardo gives the needle a flick and takes aim.

"Don't miss," I laugh.

He looks up with a cheeky grin and in it goes. "Bull's-eye!"

I can't honestly imagine the injection will make the blindest bit of difference, but it's made her happy and given her hope at least.

Ze tells us that Ricardo would like to say grace. So we adopt the pose and close our eyes for the brief blessing of the table.

"For what we are about to receive, may the Lord make us truly thankful. Amen."

But Ricardo continues to say grace in Portuguese for nearly ten minutes. Halfway through the second half of his sermon, I open my right eye and make left eye contact with Eva as we play footsie under the table until the sermon finally comes to an end.

"Amen," says everyone.

"Hallelujah!" I shout, and I mean it.

Ricardo looks pleased as I fill each glass with the blood of the pilgrim and we toast. *"Buen camino. . . . Über Alles!"* I shout out loud.

God knows where that bit came from, but Eva gives me quite a strange look. Never mind, everybody's happy, well almost.

The door bangs loudly and a big grizzly misérable head pops in.

"We are trying to sleep next door," he moans, then slams the door behind him. For about ten seconds we keep it down until Swiss John shrieks excitedly about his Moorish church extravaganza.

Two minutes later, le misérable is banging on the door again, poking his sour face in, looking even blearier eyed.

"Can you *please* keep the noise down?" he moans.

"You should have brought some earplugs, mate; this is dinnertime, not bedtime for Christ's sakes!" I tell him, and he disappears out of sight.

At the end of the meal, Ricardo gives us all a special wristband, and Ze explains what we must do. So I tie the blue band around Eva's strong wrist and tie it tight. She does the same for me, and we all make a wish. Ze explains that we must wear the band until it drops off, otherwise the wish will never come true. We all agree and wish.

"Be careful what you wish for!" shrieks Swiss John.

I look across at Eva and raise one eyebrow, and she flashes me a foxy look as she shuts her eyes with a dirty great big grin on her face.

After dinner I try in vain to coax the amigos out for a few beers, but they are happy to hang around the hostel and be good pilgrims.

So Eva, Alyssa, Sonja, and I end the night outside the bar opposite the hostel. When it is my round for the beers, I come back to find Eva being chatted up by monotone, überboring, soft-metal enthusiast Günter. I'm not worried, mind you, as he couldn't charm the pants off a dead chipmunk.

The taxi traveling, mummified, seat-stealing German erbert.

I leave them to it for a while and end up drinking with a drunken Benny Hill look-alike German wearing a button-popping safari outfit, with a big cheerful rosy-red freckled face.

We end the night with an Irish coffee courtesy of Theo, who wants me to sing "The Wild Rover." After his bidding, I take the harmonica from my pocket and blast out "Dirty Old Town" and the theme to *The A-Team*, to raucous applause echoing down the narrow streets of Mansilla. I then follow it up by the theme song to my favorite film, *The Great Escape*.

We finish up by singing a fitting rendition of the traditional Irish favorite "Seven Drunken Nights," of which I can only remember three and a half verses. Halfway through the third verse, the window opens from the hostel above and the grayhead misérable from the kitchen shouts down to us: "Can you keep the noise down? We are trying to sleep up here!"

"But you have plenty of time to sleep when you are dead!" shouts Swiss John as the window slams shut!

"But he has, hasn't he? Yes, yes, and yes!" he says excitedly, and we all piss our pants laughing. At one minute to ten, we pile back into the foyer and surprisingly into an even bigger and noisier party. No one has come to lock us in, so we carry on regardless. At one point I find myself dancing salsa with Chantel and doing a knee- and chest-slapping German dance with Benny "On Safari" Hill.

I can't remember climbing into bed that night, but the Three Amigos can.

As my head hit the pillow, I sighed longingly.

*"Buenas noches, señorita"*—which they all found most amusing.

MANSILLA DE LAS MULAS TO LEÓN

# DR. HAROLD

IF JESUS HAD TURNED UP LAST NIGHT, he would have turned the wine back into water, that's for sure. Seven drunken nights? It's more like every drunken night at the moment. I jump down off my bed and my brain rattles in my head like a pea in a tin.

"Morning, Eddie!" shouts Chantel, the large French girl, as she excitedly banters on about last night's frivolities.

"Oh, and thank you for the necklace," she says, waving a wooden T-shaped cross at me.

Could have been worse. *At least it wasn't a pearl necklace I gave her,* I think to myself.

"See you in León!" she shouts happily.

* * * *

As I wobble out onto the strange road I wonder what the next city has in store for me. León. I like the sound of León, maybe because of the film *Léon* or the Kings of Leon, a great rock band. I guess it just sounds like a cool place. I join up with Sonja on the outskirts of the city, and we both get lost until Sonja spots minute yellow arrows drawn on a wall with a small crayon, directing us to a monastery in the city center.

It's another clinical, crisp building with separate dorms for men and women, lest there be any temptation, I suppose.

Not that I have that problem, as the man sitting on the bed squashed up next to mine is yet another look-alike—this time for Britain's most prolific serial killer, Dr. Harold Shipman. Only German.

On my leisurely stroll into town, I meet Ned "Okily Dokily" Flanders and his tedious buddies.

"*Buen camino*, brother pilgrim!" they all shout, waving like fools

"Hey, come and join us," says the troublesome trio.

So I sit with them for a while but find myself being drained of energy yet again, because I tire quickly of their boring chit-chat. I feign illness and tell them I need to find the chemist straight away!

The surge of negative energy from the trio worries me for the future and I feel doomed and depressed all of a sudden. So I phone Powelly in San Francisco. He's bound to cheer me up.

"Eddie Rock, man! When are you coming to see me?" he shouts down the phone like a lunatic.

"Could be soon, mate," I tell him.

"How's life then? Some Russian gangster has shot me fucking

boat and sank the bastard!" he yells down the phone.

"Life as usual then," I joke.

"I fucking need you out here, man."

Steve goes on to tell me his latest news, and my depression lifts at his unbelievable stories of lunacy from the States.

"As soon as I'm finished, I'm there," I tell him, delighted.

* * * *

On the way back to the monastery I see a few familiar faces dotted around but not any of my amigos. I enjoy a simple pilgrim meal alone in a small bar near to the monastery followed by a few large brandies in preparation for bedding down with Dr. Harold.

# BUDDHA SHAKAMOONIE

ABSOLUTELY TERRIBLE DREAMS, and I wake with a jolt to find Dr. Harold staring down at me, telling me it's seven o'clock in the morning.

Fuck's sake.

In my desperation to get back on the road, I manage to get hopelessly lost, right outside the monastery. So I aim for the cathedral spire and pick up some arrows for a while and then find nothing except for a ghostlike pilgrim looking equally lost.

*"Hola. ¿Dónde esta el Camino, por favor, señor?"* I ask in perfect Spanish.

"Oh, you're English," he says, unimpressed.

"Any ideas?" I ask him.

He looks puzzled and begins pointing at buildings, then at something in his book with his finger to his lip, while mumbling the street names and getting nowhere fast. I get a glimpse of the title of his book.

*The Confraternity of Saint James: Guide to the Camino de Santiago.*

Shit! This guy must be in the same gang as Flanders and Double Trouble. I ought to walk away right now, but we make introductions and then proceed to get incredibly lost. I've only just met this guy and already I want to strangle him as he leads me astray. First down one street, then back, then down another, until I feel like pulling the weirdo's guide out of his hands, punching him in the face, and kicking it onto the roof of the railway station. So I refer to my own professional guide and soon find my bearings. My map says it goes this way and his says it goes that way and my patience has worn thin, so we march off in different directions, meeting up again about a mile down the road. We have breakfast in a small café on the edge of an industrial estate as Dave tells me his story.

He comes from Marsden in West Yorkshire, but his family is Catholic Irish, so we have a lot in common. Today is his first day on the Camino; I did think he looked a bit fresh.

Back on the trail, Dave starts translating the political graffiti on all the walls. His Spanish is quite good and much better than mine.

We eventually part company up the road, as he wants to look in some boring little church in his guide, and I realize I forgot to ask him who or what exactly the Confraternity of Saint James is all about. Maybe it's like the religious wing of the ramblers' association or some twisted Camino cult?

I've never been a great fan of organized religion, but I did try Buddhist meditation once. My friend and I decided to go to one of the classes held weekly in an old school building on Rowland Road in Scunthorpe. We figured that smoking a large joint of purple haze on the way there would help the meditation process along. This proved to be our undoing, because we spent most of the session bursting into fits of uncontrollable laughter. When we eventually calmed down, we sat at the back of the lively group and began chatting with other enlightened beings. Then all of a sudden, *ping*, a loud bell rang and a small Buddhist monkess glided into the room as if on roller skates reminding me of Tripitaka from *Monkey*.

*Ping* went the bell again and the whole group began chanting.

The only bit of it I remember before crumbling into fits of laughter was the classic line, "In the space before me, is the living Buddha Shakamoonie."

"The Buddha Shakamoonie? Where?"

At this point my friend was laughing so bad she had to leave the room, eventually returning straight-faced five minutes later as the whole group began to meditate.

OK, here goes. I closed my eyes and focused on my breathing . . . in and out, blowing out bad energy . . . and in with the good. Suddenly a car alarm went off in the street, followed by . . . "Fuck this and fuck that," the sound of a bottle being kicked along the ground, and its inevitable smash as a gang of youths pass by. I opened my eyes, and it looked like everyone got the hang of it all except me, so I closed my eyes and tried again.

*Huuuuuuuuchhhh putt.* A heavy smoker coughed up his lungs as he passed by the window, propelling them onto the pavement and making me feel sick.

*Ping.*

After the meditation we discussed the reincarnation process, some of which actually made sense. I loved the idea that scumbags are reincarnated and returned to earth as cockroaches or maggots, enlightened beings go to a heavenlike place and never come back to earth, while others are reincarnated again and come back as people.

But there was one question that was niggling me.

"So, where does Jesus come into all this then?" I asked the monkess.

"Good question," she said.

"Jesus himself was a Buddha, just like Shakamoonie," she answered.

"Shakamoonie is that Buddha's last name?" I asked.

"So, what's Jesus's last name?" asked my stoned friend.

"And when is he coming back?" I asked her.

"I met an angel once," I told them, and even the monkess frowns as the session veerstotally off course.

*Ping, ping, ping.* She rang the bell herself this time and breathed a sigh of relief.

End of debate!

They weren't a bad lot, really, but that was our first and last time at the class. I never knew that Buddha had a last name. So what is Jesus's last name? Christ, I suppose?

* * * *

Back on track again, and the strange, monotonous song emerges from the depths of my insane brain.

*"Old woman, old woman, are you fond of dancing?"*

*"Yes sir, yes sir, I am fond of dancing."*

Where in the name of Saint James has that lunacy come from?

The harder I try to banish it from my mind, the louder it becomes, and I begin to wonder if I'm losing my marbles. Never mind, though, I'll soon be in the U. S. of A. "Yeehar!" I shout, crossing the lovely old bridge of Puente de Órbigo. I stop for a while to rest my aching body against the cool stone to read my guidebook.

This bridge here has been the scene of many violent confrontations, including a battle between the Swabians and the Visigoths. Sounds more like a punch-up between two indie bands, if you ask me. But most famous is how the bridge gained its nickname, El Passo Honroso, the honorable passage.

The story goes that Leónese knight Don Suero de Quiñones persuaded nine of his friends to join him in challenging travelers and adventurers who dared cross the bridge to joust against them. The dandy don had declared himself imprisoned by his love for a certain young lady, and calling on Saint James as his witness, he vowed to break three hundred lances as a ransom to escape from his prison of love. Over thirty days, between the tenth of July and ninth of August 1434, the don and his Leónese knights vanquished French, Italian, German, Portuguese, and Spanish contenders. When the contest was over, they all went to Santiago de Compostela, and the young lady he loved ditched him for one of his better-looking friends.

Serves him right, really.

* * * *

I arrive in Hospital de Órbigo in a good mood. I can't stop thinking about an adventure in America. I can't wait to get this Camino finished and make tracks for San Francisco. It's gonna be great! I'll get a Harley-Davidson and meet Californian girls, full of free love! I'm digging it already, as they say.

I find the medieval pilgrims' hostel at the top of the street and enter into a lovely old courtyard with battered settees and a calm air about the place. Unfortunately the sleeping quarters are authentically medieval too, and now I know how Joseph and Mary must have felt back in Bethlehem all those years ago. All we need is some shepherds and three wise men to turn up and we're there. The shower is comparable to standing under a toy watering can in a cowshed. I drop my soap and watch it slide out of the shower under the door and into the courtyard to God knows where. So I cut my shower short, as I fear someone might go arse over tit on my soap and another Camino cut short due to injury. After the shower I venture up to the shops and find that the local store sells a fantastic array of medieval costumes. I seriously consider buying one, as anything would be an improvement on the costume I have on today. Maybe I could buy the knight's suit and Eva a Wench outfit and . . . ?

Back at the hostel I get talking to a fat American teenager sporting an Abraham Lincoln–style goat beard and wearing a huge American football top. He tells me he just started the Camino today, and he cracks open a bottle of wine to celebrate his good fortune. It's gone in under three minutes, and JJ, as he likes to be called, is high-fiving and ready for another bottle. The more he tells me about America, the more I want to go. "Everything is bigger in America," says JJ, and that's a fact! JJ is the fattest person I've met so far, and halfway through the second bottle, the conversation veers totally off course as he starts talking about *Buffy the Vampire Slayer*, monster trucks, and Taco Bell. Luckily, Eva and Dave walk in, followed by the three wise amigos and a jolly Frenchman called René. During dinner René shows me a hand-painted book of watercolors from the various stages of the Camino, including lovely pictures of wildflowers, scenery, and the bridge we just crossed today. After the meal, everybody goes for mass in the church next door, with Ninja Dave leading the way doing the wishy-washy-crossy-handy thing while bowing and nodding at strategically placed statues. At the end of the ceremony everyone goes up to the altar for Holy Communion, but I hang back this time. I just don't get what any of it means. How can people become so brainwashed by it all and believe that their religion is better than someone else's? I just don't get it. Not to mention all the wars it causes. Nowadays, poor-old Joseph and Mary would be on *Jerry Springer* or some other daytime dross, I can just imagine it!

*This week on* The Jerry Springer Show:
    "Pregnant but still a virgin!"
    We meet Nazareth couple Joseph and Mary.
    "So how has this come about, Mary?" asks Springer. "You're a virgin but you're having a baby?" He winks back at the audience.
    "Jerry, Jerry; Jerry, Jerry!" The crowd goes wild.
    "And, Joseph, do you believe her?" asks Jerry as the crowd goes boooo.
    "Well, I did do for a start, Jerry, and then when the boy was born, a load of shepherds and three wise men turned up. So I don't know what to think anymore, to be honest, Jerry."
    After the break we find out the results of the paternity test.

# LEAD US NOT INTO TEMPTATION

IN THE DISTANCE is the remarkable sight of Eva in tight tennis shorts. "Come on, let's catch up to her," says Dave, quickening his pace.

Before long I can't get a word in edgeways, as Dave bombards her with every question under the sun. There was me playing it cool and now here he is, giving it his best shot, and to make matters worse she's lapping it up. All the groundwork I put in and now to lose her to him, as she laughs at all his jokes and boring stories. I've been here before with Cocker and Belen, so I speed up and leave them to it for a while.

I smoke a cigarette and wait for them on the steps of Astorga cathedral as Monster-Truck-Vampire-loving JJ waddles past, eating a huge tortilla while slurping from a three-liter Coke bottle.

Buffet-slaying fat bastard!

He doesn't even notice me as he fills his fat face, and it feels like I've been bitten right on my knackersack by a medieval mattress mite. "Great!"

The two lovebirds arrive, fluttering all over each other, and we go inside the cathedral for a look around. Dave immediately starts doing his annoying crossy-handy thingy, kneeling and bowing all over the place.

"Who teaches you to do all this ninja shit, man?" I ask him.

"The priests teach you," says Dave, studying his guidebook.

"Yeah, right!"

"I used to be a choirboy," he says, leading us up the aisle.

"That doesn't surprise me one bit," I sigh.

On top of the excitement of the cathedral, they now want to visit the flaming museum next door.

I can't be bothered and I'm beginning to get fed up with all this shit, so I sit, guarding their packs. They play mister and missus in the museum, and an hour or so later they eventually appear, all happy and touchy-feely.

"Anyone fancy a beer?" says Dave, reveling in his ever-growing ability to charm Eva's pants down.

"Yes!" I almost shout.

Inside the bar we get stuck into some San Miguel and a whiskey chaser for the road, all courtesy of Dave. I suppose he's not such a bad lad, really. I normally like to leave my drinking until I've finished, but today can't do any harm, I shouldn't imagine. I probably need one or two to help me cope with listening to his bullshit all day long.

On leaving Astorga, Dave does the usual and gets us hopelessly lost.

I wish he would just lose his stupid book instead of us all the time.

The fucking tool! As he stares gormlessly into his blue guide, my hands itch in frustration and I realize that I've left my gloves back at the bar. It's all Dave's fault, the knob-head.

With the help of my professional guidebook, we get back on track again. Dave is telling Eva about his recent trip to Ireland, where he kissed the Blarney Stone; his trip to India, where he kissed lepers; and his trip to Indochina, where he visited a holy temple and kissed a golden monkey. What have I got to match that?

Wild West–style brawls? Drug experiments? Motorcycle accidents?

How about the time I got deported from Australia, including being escorted onto the plane in handcuffs by two armed federal police? She'd love that story! Or maybe the time I got thrown off a nightclub balcony and ended up flat on my back in an inflatable swimming pool full of foam with a naked stripper wrestling a naked dwarf. But the best part of that story was . . . Or the time I shot the paper delivery girl with my mate's air rifle! Maybe not?

It's getting hotter and hotter and my hands are itching like mad, thanks to Dave the rave and his crap guidebook. In the village of Murias de Rechivaldo, the arrows evaporate into thin roasted air. A car pulls up nearby and super Dave demonstrates his cunnilinguistic abilities to the occupants. *"Perdóneme, señor,"* he begins, guidebook at the ready. *"Dónde esta el albergue, por favor?"*

The locals in the car laugh and joke with clever clogs, who keeps looking back at us, smiling and nodding knowingly with a smug look on his face, until finally the locals announce that the next hostel is over twenty kilometers away! That wiped the stupid smile off Dave's face, I can tell you.

So with that, we follow dispirited Dave slowly out of town with talk of rain forests and rare butterflies. I want to talk about customised motorbikes and war films as he tells Eva about pygmies' pointed cocks somewhere in the Amazon jungle. Pygmies' pointed cocks! Where does he get it all from? On the desolate track, Eva tells us she needs the ladies' room, so I seize the moment and march off as Dave turns his back and shuts his eyes. The whiskey has dulled my many pains, and I feel invincible as my pace quickens to a steady jog with my arms pumping the poles, propelling me farther and farther to freedom as I plow up the track toward the ancient village on the horizon.

A gap appears in the high stone wall complete with yellow arrows.

In the old stone courtyard I throw down my pack, and as luck would have it, I find myself straight outside the old pilgrims' shelter.

"Twenty kilometers, my arse!" The Spanish locals have got a wicked sense of humor, joking with our pale-faced companion. I'll give them that for nothing. I book into the hostel and take a wander up the ancient street. I find Eric sitting on a stone slab outside the old bar, drinking a large glass of beer and smoking a roll-up. He shows me a pebble he's brought with him from Belgium and explains the ancient tradition of bringing a stone from home to place at the Cruz de Ferro, the highest point of the Camino, high in the mountains.

Inside the old bar a group of Americans are having a good-old time drinking whiskey and beer. One of them is an absolute dead ringer for Ronnie Drew, the famous singer from the Dubliners, with his two-tone beard and soft eyes, and his bearded pals wouldn't look out of place swinging their pants at a beatnik folk festival.

I see Dave wandering up the old cobbled street toward me. "How come you stopped here, then?" he asks.

"It's as good a place as any, I suppose, plus I just met Ronnie Drew from the Dubliners. He's walking the Camino with his wife; he's going to sing a few songs later on," I lie.

Dave can't believe his luck, and I can't believe he believed my bullshit, but he is quite gullible, it seems. He goes inside in search of Ronnie as I walk back to the hostel and spot Eva in the queue for the showers. She says a quiet hello as I pass, and I don't know what to say to her anymore with pale face on the scene. I'm certainly not playing second fiddle to him, that's a fact! I grab my towel and wash kit from upstairs and fall in behind Eva in the queue.

Eventually the shower is free and she goes in, reappearing seconds later with a dirty great big grin on her face.

"There are two showers in here; I don't mind if you don't. We are all pilgrims, after all," she says.

The hostel owner shrugs his opinion, so I follow her inside the steamy room and we strip naked. It seems like my wish has come true!

I leave Eva getting dried off and take one last look at her naked arse as I head out the door. All this showering has left me with quite a thirst.

\* \* \* \*

Back at the bar . . .

"Ronnie Drew," laughs Dave, gesturing to the bearded Americans

"Where's Eva?" he sighs, next to a pile of empty beer bottles.

"Eva has just got out the shower, David," I say, ruffling my wet hair.

"Oh, did you see her?" he asks.

"Yeah, you could say that," I say with raised eyebrows.

Eva joins us moments later and asks me for a cigarette.

"I didn't know you smoked!" says Dave in a shocked, effeminate voice.

"I only smoke when I'm drinking, or after sex." She laughs in a husky Marlene Dietrich kind of way.

We see out the end of the night, sitting on the grass with Eric and the Dubliner doppelgangers with a large carry-out from the bar. Needless to say, the blood of the pilgrim flows freely.

# TOMAS THE TEMPLAR

DAVE EMERGES FROM HIS SLEEPING BAG looking like he's just pecked his way out of an egg. My head feels as fragile as an egg, my brain has shrunk to almost the same size, and it takes us almost an hour to get ready.

"Fuck me, how much did we have to drink last night?" says Dave.

"I don't know. I think I'm still drunk."

Eventually we stagger out onto the road and get caught up in a procession of fresh faces coming from Astorga. One of them is a highly excitable South African girl with crazy eyes, giving a running commentary about everything she sees, hears, feels, and does.

"Her and Swiss John in the same room? Forget about it!"

On top of my savage hangover, other strange sensations are

beginning to manifest down the front of each of my legs, and I am not the only one to go through an odd metamorphosis. Now Dave's face reminds me of Ronald McDonald, as somehow his lips have swelled to twice the normal size and are luminous and shining like a baboon's arse. It cheers me up for a split second until I feel a sharp stabbing pain down the shins of both my legs, unlike any other. At first I put it down to shin splints and shrug it off, hoping it will go away with my hangover, but minutes later my walk turns into a very painful limp.

In Rabanal del Camino we stop for breakfast before the steep climb to the Cruz de Ferro, the highest point of the Camino. What a day to start with a new injury!

As we begin the steep climb, both my legs start to lock up, and like the drunken fools we are, we have run out of water. Dave starts to fuss at me like an old lady, and I feel a bit guilty about sneaking back into the room last night and putting a heavy stone in the bottom of his pack. But he gets us lost again, and I soon change my mind, even more so as he gets his blue guidebook out and a finger goes to his inflatable big red lips as he looks for yellow arrows.

"Ah," he says. "Past the Iron Cross stands a pilgrims' hostel. It's run by a member of the Knights Templar called Tomás, and that's where we will spend the night. It says here that 'Knights Templar Tomás is famous for chaining himself to the railings of the electricity board in downtown León when they turned off his power", says Dave excitedly.

"Nice one," I tell him. "I can't wait to meet him. He sounds like a rebel and an outlaw, and I bet he's a top geezer." That thought alone spurs me onward despite the pain. My legs are swelling like balloons and very painful to touch. Now I am starting to worry. I don't know what the hell is wrong with me. The only saving grace is Tomás and the fact that we're walking on tarmac and not on rocks. So I count my blessings and crack on. I try out a variety of new walking techniques, including sliding my feet, walking sideways, then dangerously backward, but nothing helps in any way.

Eventually we reach the Iron Cross.

At first glance it looks more like a pilgrims' rubbish dump than a thousand-year-old shrine, with old shoes, cigarettes, mass cards, a sock, an old hat, and rosary beads littering up the place. I wonder if there's a syringe full of morphine Sellotaped somewhere to get me to the next hostel.

I take my pebble and drop it on the ground as Dave looks skyward, saying "Hail Mary" five times for my stricken legs. I scramble down the rocks, and shooting pains travel from my legs to my brain and out my mouth.

We rest for a while on the grass and laugh as a young German arrives with the biggest, roundest rock on his shoulders. He clambers up the stones, and with a triumphant thud, the rock hits the ground, stops for a split second, then begins to roll back down again.

"What a fucking douche," I say to Dave as we watch him struggle again, only this time he places it carefully and jacks a few small rocks around it. At last triumphant! "Yeah, well done, you silly bastard," I joke, and turn to Dave.

"So if he does exist, do you think that God will favor he who places the biggest stone any more than someone who only brought a pebble?"

He thinks about it for a moment.

"Well, the meek shall inherit the earth," he says sagely.

"If you say so, Dave," I tell him as he throws on his pack.

"Ooh eck, these straps are cutting right into my shoulders," he moans.

"Mine did that at first," I tell him.

"No, it's strange, but my pack feels heavier," he says, puzzled.

"It's all that wine we had last night, mate."

* * * *

The descent into Manjarín is a nightmare beyond belief. I feel shooting pains with every step, and then every so often a lightning bolt of pain stops me literally in my tracks, leaving me gasping for breath.

Eventually we enter the abandoned village, keeping a keen eye out for its famous occupant and our savior, Tomás the Templar. At first it looks like the village children have made quite an impressive play den, with a ramshackle watchtower made of planks of wood, rocks, and tarpaulins, with rope and string holding it all together. But didn't he say "abandoned village"?

"This is it," says Dave, befuddled with excitement.

"What!"

At Casa Tomás an old table is set for dinner, and miserable-looking pilgrims lie slumped in flea-bitten settees, swatting flies, with looks of "we were here first" and "we're better mates with Tomás than you are" on their smug faces.

There's a clapped-out Mercedes in the drive, and it looks like Tomás has guests. The legend finally appears dressed in jungle fatigues with crosses, ornaments, and crystals slung around his neck like Mr. T. of *The A-Team*—only a third the size, but with that same crazy fool look about him. He doesn't look happy and keeps refilling his glass from a bottle on the table. I can't look away from the bottle, as satanic flies buzz around my eyes, ears, and mouth. Funnily enough, Tomás is strangely unaffected by them.

*"Perdón, señor,"* says Dave. *"¿Donde esta los servicios?*

Tomás scoffs grumpily. *"¡Donde!"* gesturing to the surrounding fields

"Don-day? What's that supposed to mean, Dave?" I ask.

"Anywhere," he says, as five bluebottles land on his big glistening lips. So no toilet, and by the look of Tomás, there are no showers either! Flies land on my lips, in my ears, on my scabby hands, and in my eyes. I smoke the world's fastest cigarette and angrily stamp the butt into the ground as intense pain shoots through my fragile body and mind!

"Aaaaaaaaaaaaaaaaagggggghhhhhhhhhhhhhh! Fuck this fucking bastarding shithole!" I scream.

"But, but, but, where are you going?" says stuttering Dave, as I grab my pack and limp away.

"Anywhere but here!"

"But, but, but!"

"You can stay here with Lord of the Fucking Flies! I'm off," I tell him

"But your legs," he says.

"It's not my fucking legs, Dave! It's my fucking head," I say, hobbling slowly away, closely followed by a buzzing black cloud.

"But where are you going?" he says.

"AS FAR AWAY FROM THIS SHITHOLE AS POSSIBLE!"

* * * *

Now, according to Dave's book we are ten kilometers or so from the next pilgrims' shelter, and as long as it's not run by Tomás, I don't care. I'm nearing the end of my sanity all in one day and I'm worried, very worried. My head is all jumbled up and I feel feverish and dizzy.

The descent from the mountain is an absolute nightmare, and we pass some very strange rodent-type people shuffling along. The rodent man has a rat-tail hairdo, which I deem suits his face and probably his personality, and his rodent partner just looks like an albino chipmonk with pink eyes. Their strangeness is confirmed, as they totally ignore our friendly salutations with dull, sour looks.

To add insult to injury, my hands start itching like crazy! Luckily, inspiration comes in many forms—in this case, a jolly one-legged man on crutches and the bouncing breasts of his happy blonde companion fly past us, giving me new hope for a few minutes, until a sharp pain has me cursing in five different languages.

The hostel appears to be flyless and also has a very nice bar and restaurant. So we celebrate our immediate arrival with refreshing tankards of San Miguel. As soon as we get a couple of beers into us, Dave's incessant worrying flicks from my legs to wondering where Eva is. He doesn't have to wait long before she arrives. She's wondering whether or not to carry on to the hostel in Molinaseca, not far down the road. But before she has time to think, Dave buys her a large beer, helps her off with her pack, and plonks her between us on a solid oak stool.

I'm in no mood for drinking or listening to any more bullshit, so I leave them to it. Ten minutes later I find myself a nice bottom bunk in the quickly filling dormitory.

The Dutch harmonica appreciation society have reappeared loitering with intent around the showers, of which I'm third in line. When it's finally my turn, one of the Dutch duo decides to wash her underwear in the sink. I curse and holler as I get blasts of freezing-cold water, then scalding-hot, sending my mind over the edge yet again.

As I exit the shower, she's standing there waiting with her towel. I smile nicely at her as I pass and wait till I can hear the angelic singing and splashing from within. Time for a bit of religious education!

*Fight fire with fire!* I think to myself as I twiddle the taps.

First one way, then the other, then back again.

"Ooooh! Aaaaagh! *Godverdommer!*" she wails.

Her screams and sobs are music to my burned, blistered ears, and I smile innocently as she emerges all red-faced, huffing and puffing.

"Lovely shower, isn't it?" I muse as she passes me by without even a look.

The rat couple arrives on the scene, sniffing at everything and everyone with distrust as they search for beds. Thankfully the South African girls are full of life, and we strike up a bit of banter in Dutch Afrikaans. The excitable girl we met earlier is traveling with her mother and a few friends. She is louder than Theo and ten times more excitable than Swiss John, and completely off her head; her actions reminding me of a clockwork toy.

* * * *

Back down in the bar, Dave and Eva are getting harassed by a drunken farmer in blue overalls covered in cow shit. He looks remarkably like David Icke, the Premier League goalkeeper who turned conspiracy theorist, believing that members of the British monarchy are, in fact, lizards from outer space that feed on homeless children.

Dave and Eva look worried as Icke stands before them, wobbling and swaying with pontoon eyes, making inappropriate remarks and gestures. The stout barman shouts and waves the yellow card at the drunken farmer, who then twists his double-glazed features, all serious and menacing for a moment, but with wobble and a shrug he sits down and lights a Ducados with his laughing cronies. Eva decides it's time for a shower, and as she leaves, our eyes fall upon her peachy tight ass.

"I think I love her," says Dave with a longing sigh.

I feel like telling him about the steamy shower I had with her and that I love her too, and then I'll challenge him to a duel at dawn. But I can hardly walk, never mind fight. So we get drunk instead, and I give him a major inquisition about his ridiculous religious beliefs.

In the middle of the night I hear screams and shouts in the darkness. The lights go on, and all the commotion is based around Dave sitting bolt upright in his bunk, screaming like a banshee with his hand on chest, setting in motion a chain of pandemonium. The clock work girl is screaming, her mother is screaming, the rat people are screaming, the Dutch women are screaming!

"What the fucking hell is going on?"

Dave is muttering, stuttering, and clutching his chest, and

at first I wonder if he's been stabbed, and by whom! I see blood between his fingers and a kind of slime. As he calms down, I pry his shaking hand away from his chest, where the flattened remains of a lizard slide down his stomach and settle in his crotch.

I don't know who I feel sorry for the most—the lizard or the slayer.

# JUDAS ROCK

A VERY SEXY FRENCH GIRL has monopolized the bathroom, and her older companion states knowingly that she will be in there awhile. Eventually she comes out looking like some kind of model for the designer walking-clothes industry, and reptile killer Dave's eyes pop out of his shrunken head, giving him the added incentive to stop moaning about lizards and hangovers and get ready for the road.

It's a lovely, fresh morning, but I can't escape the pain both physical and mental as repetitive-song syndrome takes hold once again.

"Every step I take, every move I make," I mumble over and over again as the song by the Police keeps running through my troubled mind. I hobble past a memorial stone for yet another poor soul who never made it to Santiago, and I wonder if I'll actually make it myself. Dave is totally doing my head in, fussing all over me like an old lady and offering to carry my pack. Thankfully, he gets the message and walks off in front of me with a nice Spanish lady. I keep my mind off the pain by listening in to their conversation, and from what I can gather, they are talking about the cities of Spain—Madrid, Barcelona, and Seville. Which ones are the biggest and have the biggest and best churches, the biggest swimming pools, the most people, and other highly boring statistics. Surely, if you go through all the trouble of learning a foreign language, the least you could do is find something interesting to talk about.

With every step I take and every move I make comes more pain. My legs are unrecognizably swollen, but luckily the next hostel is close by, so I think I'll find a quiet bar to chill, drink, and think about what on earth I'm going to do next. I tell Dave to go on ahead, but he won't leave me—until the sexy French catwalk model and her older companion walk past. Dave's eyes light up and the fussing stops.

"¡Hola, Josephine! ¡Hola, Delacroix!" he says, delighted.

"Is he her boyfriend?" I ask.

"Oh no, that's her father!" he says.

"Not tonight, Josephine?" I laugh.

"What?"

The Napoleonic joke goes way over his head. He's just too interested in following her spectacular tits and arse all the way to Santiago. Silver-tongued cavalier Dave wastes no time in small talk. In the space of ten minutes he's told her his life story, and he knows her life story, her phone number, and email. Now he's talking about visiting her in Paris and then afterward visiting the pope in Rome! I can't believe what I'm hearing—his bullshit is almost comical. They split from Papa and head off into the distance, deep in captivating conversation. A gunshot shatters the peace, then another, then several, and I wonder if someone has pushed in one queue too many. As I struggle down the mountain track, more rapid gunshots comes from the valley below. Could it be a total pilgrim wipeout down there?

In the distance I spot Dave, his fiancée, and his future father-in-law sitting and waiting for me beside an old bridge; after a quick photo shoot we sadly part company with Delacroix and Josephine.

"We'll meet again; don't know where, don't know when, but we will," says Dave to Josephine as she walks away, smiling and blowing kisses like Audrey Hepburn. Dave waves like a fool with tears in his eyes.

"Go and join them. Don't let me spoil your fun," I tell him.

"No, I can't leave you like this," he says.

So we stroll into town and take coffee. Soon after Eva arrives and immediately starts fussing all over me, wanting to give me a leg massage, which is exactly the last thing I need right now. I can hardly touch my legs, never mind massage them. The pair of them start twittering and flapping and offering to carry my pack and get a bus or a taxi or . . .

"Will you just leave me alone!" I shout at them.

"We're only trying to help you," says Dave.

"We can wait for you in Ponferrada," says Eva.

"Please just go," I plead. "I'll be OK. Don't worry."

They head off into the distance, obviously discussing my problems, and they keep looking back with worried looks on their faces as I limp off in search of a chemist.

\* \* \* \*

"Santa Maria," says the chemist, looking skyward and saying five Hail Marias at the same time.

"Tendonitis," she adds, prodding at my tree-trunk legs. "Rest up for a week or two and the swelling will go."

Rest up for a couple of weeks? *Where?* I wonder.

I follow the yellow arrows to the hostel with po-faced misérables loitering with intent around every exit and entry. They view me with fear, suspicion, and contempt as I approach, limping painfully.

I take one look at them and one look at the big yellow arrow and decide it's Ponferrada or bust.

I walk steadily out of town with my harmonica blasting away and propelling me slowly forward; even in terrible pain I manage to learn a new tune: Billy Joel's "Piano Man."

I'm soon in Ponferrada and come to rest in a modern plaza.

People stare and women steer their children away to safety while I laugh like a madman, because I know I look absolutely terrible. As per usual I lose sight of the arrows, ending up in a medieval plaza, and I spot Dave and Eva sitting and chatting at a café.

"Shit." I leap back out of sight. *Did they see me?*

Fuck, the last thing I need is those two fussing me to death, but there's no way I can get past without them seeing me and without them doing my head in again. Twenty painful minutes later I've circumnavigated the plaza and I peep around the corner. "Shit." They are still there, and they're so close I can hear them discussing average rainfalls in Tanzania or some bollocks.

I dive back into the shadows and stand in awe at the large, imposing Knights Templar castle. Too busy staring at it, I fail

to notice that I'm also leaning on the wall of Molly Malone's
Irish Bar.

"The luck of the Irish!" I feel that a pint of Guinness may
just save the day. Several pints later I'm feeling fantastic with
my Franklin W7 Euro Translator smoking in overdrive as I try
to chat up the pretty barmaid. I tell her I'm going to America
to buy a motorbike.

Eng: *motorbike*

Esp: *moto*

She's very impressed, and I impress her some more by
playing my new song on the harmonica.

"Can you sing?" I ask her.

She blushes. *"Loco peregrino."*

Esp: *loco*

Eng: *crazy*

"Me, crazy?"

"Yes, crazy. You sing!" She laughs.

"OK, *loca chica*, maybe you know this song?"

*"We'll be going loco down in Acapulco if you stay too long.*
*Yes we'll be going loco down on the Camino.*
*The magic down here is so strong."*

In walk Dave and Eva. Both look totally unimpressed.

"We saw you in the square, you know," says Dave in a gay
voice.

"What are you doing here? Where are you staying?" asks
Eva sharply.

"I'm staying here and getting pissed! Why? Where are you
staying?"

"Oh, we don't know yet. We, err, are . . . err?" Dave starts mumbling.

I signal to the barmaid to line the drinks up, and fear appears in their eyes.

"No, no, no. Thank you!"

"You won't drink with me?" I act outraged.

"We're going to the castle," they say, hurrying out the door.

Oh well, at least I'm not sitting and minding their packs like a complete fool again

"Nobody wants to drink with me; do you want to drink with me?" I ask the gorgeous barmaid.

"Why not?" She smiles and pours herself a brandy.

Rosa is her name, and she plays me a Spanish version of the Pogues on the music system as my Franklin W7 Euro Translator starts smoking.

Eng: *beautiful*

Esp: *bonita*

Rosa blushes. "What is the word in English?" she asks.

"Beautiful."

She repeats the word over and over. "Beautiful."

I begin to wonder if Mr. Franklin should invent an upgraded version of this handy tool. Including added sections:

Drinking and smoking
Chatting up girls
Sexual liaisons
Scoring drugs
Useful swear words
Law and order

A black and red bottle on the shelf catches my eye, and Rosa brings it over for my inspection. It's a Belgian beer called Judas.

"Yep, line 'em up!" I tell her.

As I drink the last drops from the bottle, failure, fear, and uncertainty come flooding back in a tidal wave of depression. Now I feel like Judas—Judas, the anti-pilgrim—betraying my friends and betraying myself for that matter, so I buy an extra bottle of Judas, one for the road, as they say. My bar bill is best part of sixty pieces of silver. I bid farewell to bonita Rosa, and she wishes me *"Buen camino, loco peregrino."* She laughs as I hobble off in search of the pilgrims' hostel.

After an agonizing stroll in the baking-hot sun, I eventually find the hostel. In the grounds, a group of men are working on an impressive totem pole, with pilgrims instead of eagle spirits and scallop shells for coyotes. The hostelero appears and tells me to wait for Chico, and through the kitchen window I see the *Three Amigos* laughing and joking while having their daily bread. I don't want them to see me like this, and I wish I'd never bought the Judas now. It's not so funny anymore. I don't think Ricardo would see the humorous side of it, as he's wearing that Jesus T-shirt again.

Toothless Chico appears and immediately bums a cigarette off me. It looks to me that he may have had a few drinks himself, and after our smoke he gestures for me to follow him into the hostel.

Halfway up the stairs he stops to talk to someone, so I give him the slip and wander off on my own as worried, fearful faces peep out of the crowded dorms.

Beware, the Anti-Pilgrim is among you. Be afraid! I sneak unnoticed into an empty room at the end of the corridor and quietly shut the door.

*Judassssssssssssssss.* I hear the whispers coming from the corridor. Fearing the return of Chico and the painful thought of the crowded dorms in the stifling heat send me well and truly loco, loco, loco! It's only four o'clock in the afternoon, and I'm going out of my mind soaked in a feverish red-hot sweat.

*Judassssssssssssssssssssssssss* hisses through my mind.

It's time to rid myself of the evidence of Judas once and for all; so I down him in three gulps and hide the empty bottle in the wardrobe to create a bit of pilgrim intrigue and evidence that the anti-pilgrim is more than just a myth. I sneak out of the empty room and hobble back into town and find a quiet Spanish bar in the old plaza . . . and stupefy myself with whiskey.

PONFERRADA TO VILLAFRANCA DEL

BIERZO

# FEAR AND LOATHING IN PONFERRADA

THE RABID DOG SINKS HIS RANCID FANGS into my face as
I stare into its bright yellow eyes, and I find myself screaming,
sitting bolt upright in a cold sweat, and there before me stands
yet another empty bottle of Belgian premium lager. "Oh Jesus."
My fecking head is wrecking. I wish I'd have saved it till now!
Hair of the rabid dog would be just the ticket out of here!

My legs feel like concrete poles—with each thudding step
a new agony.

*Judas, Judas, Judassssss.* I hear the whispers again, hissing loud
and clear. On the way out of town I stop for a much-needed
coffee in a crowded bar, and an odd-looking girl in the corner
keeps staring at me and giving me the eye. She looks strangely

familiar, but I can't put my finger on it. As the song *Bette Davis eyes* by Kim Cairns plays on the radio, the girl looks over again.

That's it. I've got it. *She's got Johnny Vegas eyes!*

Eyes, face, the full fucking monty. It cheers me up for a millisecond as I laugh to myself. Then I cry as I wonder how much longer I can keep going. I'll crawl on my hands and knees or roll like the Indian yogi, but no taxis like Günter or Flanders—no fucking way.

If I could get my hands on some quality marching powder, that might help. But where will I get some? Maybe I can ask Johnny Vegas eyes over there, but she looks more like a cakehead than a cokehead!

* * * *

The only thing I can do is carry on painfully until I can finally go no farther. It's boiling hot and I'm out of water and delusional. If I can just make it to the bus shelter up ahead so I can get out of this heat. But with every painful step it seems to get farther and farther away, like a desert mirage, and Judas laughs in my ear once again. I finally make it to the glass shelter and find the body of Dr. Andreas and his wife, Greta, lying motionless in the buzzing heat.

"*Hola*, doctor! Are you OK?" I ask him.

He gradually opens one eye, then another.

"*Buen camino*, Eddie Rock!" He laughs and, barely alive, Greta just nods. "It is her circulation," says the doctor, "and this heat."

I explain everything to the good Dr. Andreas, who then gives my legs a quick going over with a worried look on his face.

His diagnosis is acute tendonitis, a condition where the muscles swell up around the ligaments and stop them from working properly. The only known cure for it is good-old R and R.

To help me get to the next hostel, the good doctor gives me two of his special painkillers. I don't even ask what they are and neck them down with a gulp of water from the fountain. I rest in the scorching heat, drifting in and out of consciousness.

A magpie settles in the tree close by.

"One for sorrow," I murmur dreamily.

"What is that?" asks Greta, opening her eyes.

"Oh, it's just a saying. When you see a magpie, it's one for sorrow, two for joy."

"And for three?" she asks.

"Three for a girl and four for a boy," I tell her.

Greta is in hysterics. It seems laughter is the best medicine after all, and we seize this moment of joviality and hit the road.

Up ahead is the familiar sight of Eric smoking a roll-up by the side of the trail. I pat him on the back and sit down beside him, and then we both jump back in amazement as I stare into the face of a complete stranger! The man looks bewildered. I'm bewildered, so I wish him a *"Buen camino"* and hit the road. I put the case of mistaken identity down to the heat and the miraculous painkilling tablets, or maybe it was the devil tricking me once again? Before long, Greta has to rest, so I bid them a farewell for now and hope to see them later in the medieval town of Villafranca del Bierzo. Luckily the hostel is the first building I come to, and an overly aggressive German woman with a mustache and a man's voice tells me I'm number twelve in her queue.

"Do I look like I give a fuck?" I snarl in true anti-pilgrim style.

Her frog-like eyes almost pop out of her stupid face as I limp away before she can inflict anymore psychological damage on me.

The hostelera returns from her lunch, and all hell breaks loose as a new hard-core group of Polish pilgrims swarm the check-in, intent on total hostel monopolization without mercy!

The German woman stands with her hands on her hips, outraged, as a kindly old English pilgrim turns to me and quietly says that the Poles have their packs taken by minibus each day. They are phony pilgrims. "Bogus," he whispers with a wink.

**\* \* \* \***

I limp down to the telephone booth to phone Steve in San Fran. I need a bit of cheering up, but his wife answers and says that Steve is in Alameda County jail again . . . and won't be out for quite some time.

"What!"

"They took him away wrapped in a Velcro blanket," she says.

"What the fuck!"

"Yep, he never learns." She laughs

I can't believe it. No more land of the free! My hopes cruelly dashed yet again. I hang up in total disbelief and hobble back in a state of mental, physical, and spiritual pain.

# REST, RECUPERATION, AND STEVE IRWIN

I'M UP AT THE CRACK OF DAWN to say goodbye to all my friends, as I doubt I will ever see any of them again.

The amigos and Alyssa, Dr. Andreas and Greta, and many others who I kept up with since the beginning. I wish them all a *"Buen camino"* for the final time. Then I go back to my bedroom and to sleep, and hope for a miracle

I dream that I'm running with bulls, but back in Scunthorpe High Street, swerving through the busy streets on a cronky old red Honda C50 moped on benefit day. But suddenly the machine coughs and chugs to a halt.

"Oh fuckety-fuck, fuck, shit!" I scream in frustration as I frantically try to kick-start the piece of shit moped back to life and the snorting monsters come charging down upon me. In my desperation I shinny up the nearest lamppost, but Polish gangster rappers in loud tracksuits try to throw me off, prying my fingers from the post as the raging bulls pass below me, and one of them tries to steal my watch as I fall.

And for the second day running I wake up screaming in a cold sweat.

I feel afraid so I try praying to God, but I get the same old answer.

"The Lord helps those who help themselves." I cry to myself yet again.

But how do I help myself? In a desperate measure to heal my legs, I fill a washing tub full of icy water and stand in it, hoping that the swelling goes down, while getting an array of astonished looks and comments from a variety of pilgrims. I'm soon bored to tears, and I limp off to the nearby church of Saint James. I nod to the lady attendant reading her book and sit for a while in silence. Suddenly the peace is shattered by the sight and sound of loud foreign voices as the taxi-loving Poles swarm all over the place like noisy ants. The lady looks up from her book and frowns, and we catch each other's eye, then shake our heads, both looking upward at the same time to the same God.

I limp out of the church and head to the other pilgrims' hostel for a nose around. It's much older and nicer than the modern one, with big chestnut beams running through the building and the heavenly smell of fresh coffee coming from within. The Polish taxi is here, waiting in the street with the engine running, and a party of German children gets ready for their day. A fat, spotty, sleepy boy emerges from an old burger van, triggering a return to repetitive-song syndrome.

"Isn't it ironic? Don't ya think?" By Alanis Morissette.

The man in charge of the group reminds me of Steve Irwin,

the crocodile hunter, complete with enthusiasm, safari outfit, and handsome girlfriend, whom he can't seem to take his hands off. I go inside and get another coffee as the heavy petting reaches another level.

"Hello, Eddie!"

At the table is the big black French girl Chantel carefully bandaging her right leg. Her big face lights up and she gives me a bone-crunching hug.

"Jesus, what happened to you?" I ask her.

"I got bitten by a dog," she says sadly.

At this point, the strangest of things happens. I clearly hear my late father's voice right in my ear, saying, "I'd say the dog was more frightened than she was!"

I almost piss myself laughing on the spot and have to turn away and bite my lip, pretending I've suddenly got something in my eye.

Chantel is waiting with a group of bandaged pilgrims for the bus to come and spirit them away to the next hostel somewhere up the mountain, so I bid her a good taxi trip and whistle my way outside.

"Is dat a sea shanty you are whistling?" asks the Steve Irwin guy. "I love sea shanties!" he says excitedly.

"No, it's Alanis Morissette."

"Listen, do you know this tune?" he asks, and off he goes, whistling and conducting himself with cymbals, drums, and fireworks like Last Night of the Proms.

"No, no," I keep saying, wishing he would go away.

"OK! Now this bit you will know for sure," he says, blowing an imaginary trumpet.

"No, I don't know any sea shanties."

"This is a sea shanty," he says.

"I know it's a sea shanty; you just told me."

"Oh, so you do know a sea shanty. Are you a sailor?"

"No, I'm a carpenter."

"Just like our Lord Jesus," he beams.

"Yeah, if you say so."

"In my country our carpenters wear old-fashioned black-and-white clothes, travel around Germany learning many skills. Do you have this in your country?"

"Yes!" I lie. "Morris dancers."

"They dance?" he wonders.

"Yes, dancing carpenters."

"I will tell zat to my friends in Germany," he says as his Fräulein comes within groping distance. I wander back up the road to the church, leaving them locked in a passionate embrace.

I've never really prayed before and meant it, apart from the time when I got washed out to sea on a surfboard (twice) or while sitting around a roulette table. I kneel and get ready. Right, here goes.

"Dear Saint James, hear my pra—"

"Ya, ya, dit is good, dat is good, dit, dat, dit, dat," shouts Irwin with his Fräulein, kissing and canoodling all over the place with his groping octopus hands sliding over her body. Why all of a sudden they choose to sit directly in front of me in this great big empty church is beyond comprehension, and after an eternity of their noise and flirtatious behavior, they thankfully leave, wishing me good luck and a happy Camino. I smile weakly, thinking completely the opposite, and I make a pact with Saint James that I will not touch a drop of alcohol until I get to Santiago de Compostela. On the condition that he gets me there in one piece. "Amen!"

* * * *

Back at the empty hostel the lady in charge arrives in her car, and I show her my swollen legs. She takes pity on me and says I can stay as long as I want for no charge. She also brings my attention to a poster on the wall. It says that a nearby hostel in Ruitelán specializes in Reiki healing for tendonitis. At last a glimmer of hope fills me with joy.

But a Hungarian pilgrim overhears my plight and says he too can help me, as he is a Reiki healer. So why wait till tomorrow? The Hungarian healer gets to work on my concrete legs, and the hostelera keeps flashing me puzzled looks. I shrug and wonder what good it's actually doing me. Even the Hungarian has a worried look on his face. He finishes up and I thank him all the same and then retire to the heart of darkness with all hope shattered.

# LAST LEGS

SO MUCH FOR THAT REIKI HEALING BULLSHIT. A lot of good that did! I knew it wouldn't work. I stumble painfully out of town, and on the outskirts of Villafranca the yellow arrows disappear into thin air, and a new repetitive song plays on and on in my tired brain.

*Where's your arrow gone?"*
*Where's your arrow gone? (Where's the arrows gone?)*
*Where's the arrows gone? (Where's the arrows gone?)*
*Far, far away (Far, far, away)*
*Last night I heard my mama singing a song.*
*Ooh-we, chirpy, chirpy, cheep, cheep*
*Woke up this morning and the arrows were gone.*

Thoughts of despair and hopelessness hit me like a freight train. How much farther can I go on like this? Is it mind over matter or am I just being stupid? I don't know.

I plod painfully onward and hopefully in the right direction.

* * * *

The village reminds me a bit of where my grandparents used to live back in Ireland. The people look quite poor and obviously make the most out of what they've got. On an old stone bench a gang of old people are having some heated conversations. An ancient lady shouts at a laughing old man, and she hits him in the chest and wails in his ear as his mates laugh raucously. I pass them by, and they stop squabbling for a moment to wish me a "*¡Buen camino!*" Great characters altogether.

* * * *

Deep in a valley at the base of the mountain stands the tranquil village of Ruitelán, and I sit under the trees, soaking my legs in the cold stream, hoping yet again for some kind of anti-inflammatory miracle. My thoughts turn to despair as hard drops of rain splash through the leaves into the stream. Suddenly the sky turns black and lightning cracks nearby.

I arrive at the pilgrims' hostel soaked to the bone.

I check in and explain that I have acute tendonitis to the hostelero. He runs his thumbs down my legs and I almost hit the roof!

Now he fully agrees. He tells me to relax and not to worry, as he delves into an interesting old tea chest, producing a handful of what looks like homeopathic remedies. Before I know what's going on, he put one of the remedies in his left hand, then he takes my right hand and tells me to put my index finger and thumb together. He loops his finger through mine and tells me to squeeze hard. He pulls apart my finger and thumb easily, and then shakes his head. He tries another remedy and the same thing happens, but third time's a charm! He can't separate my fingers and states confidently, "Anacardium orientale," then places the vial in my hand.

"Two to be taken on the hour every hour, and within half an hour of coffee and food. By tomorrow you will be cured," he says with an aura of certainty.

I feel like telling him to "Pull the other one."

What I really need is some kind of strong morphine-based drug injection and nurses fussing all over me instead of all this finger pulling.

"Come and find me after dinner, and I'll fix your problem," he says.

"Thank you, I will," I tell him as I shake his hand and he introduces himself as Luis.

Another man appears, very much reminding me of the actor Anthony Quinn. He tells me his name is Carlos. He pats me on my back, shakes my hand, and laughs all at the same time. He is full of life, with an infectious laugh, and finally I'm laughing again too.

The hostel here is very beautiful and well maintained with not one misérable in sight. All exit and entry points are clear, with noise to a minimum. I like the way Carlos keeps telling me that I'm going to be cured, like he's mending a puncture on my bicycle or something.

My watch tells me it's time for my new medicine, and seconds later a couple of the little tablets dissolve on my tongue.

\* \* \* \*

Back at the stream a cat chases a barking dog and a chicken chases a screeching cat. I think the Chinese tablets are kicking in now as my stress has gone, my fear and loathing a distant memory. It starts to rain heavily again, so I retreat back to the dormitory for a lie-down. In the foyer I find Carlos pulling a laughing woman by the fingers.

\* \* \* \*

At mealtime our splendid hosts provide us with a wonderful salad starter of tuna, olives, fresh bread, and potatoes, with bottles of wine and mineral water to wash it all down. Carlos comes in and out of the room with more food and laugher while joking in his broken English, with hints of French and Spanish. I keep expecting him at any moment to grab the guitar from the corner and serenade us all with a happy song. More pilgrims squeeze onto the cramped table and everyone is polite and respectful. The homemade wine is passed freely around the table, but I stick with the water. Lead us not into temptation.

After the meal Luis shows me into his quarters and closes the door behind us.

"OK, lie down please," says Luis.

"Aurrrgggfff." I position myself onto the mattress on the floor.

"OK, now relax," he says, rubbing massage oil into my stricken legs.

"Relax," he says, but my legs feel like they are made of stone and I can't stop myself tensing them up.

"If you don't relax, I can't help you," he states sternly.

Eventually, I let go and put my trust into his healing hands. I've got a feeling this procedure could be painful, so I shut my eyes and try to calm down. It feels like he's breathing hot air onto my legs!

I open my eyes and look down, and thankfully he isn't.

"OK, does it hurt here?" he says, pressing down my shins.

"Yes!"

"And here?"

"Yes!"

It might just be easier to tell him where it doesn't hurt.

I answer yes to all his proddings and yes to all his poking, as his oily hands go back down to my feet, massaging my soles, ankles, and toes. Then in a flash, *whip!*

"Fucking hell." He's just nearly pulled my toe off and now he's at it again! Rubbing away and then . . . *yank!*

"Jesus!" It's like a violent game of this little piggy as Luis tries to pull each one of my toes quite literally off my foot!

This little piggy goes to market; this little piggy goes to— "Aarrrggggh"—a fucking torture dungeon and gets his head pulled off!

"Does this hurt? Does that hurt?"

"Yes!" I keep saying. "Yes!"

Then "NO!" I shout for the first time. At last! He's found a part of my body that doesn't hurt! He keeps on whipping my toes violently, and each time he does it, my body goes into spasm. His hands press hard in my groin, releasing the pressure, and then he's back down my leg again for more painful toe pulling.

I don't know much about this kind of thing, but it's as if he's finding the source of the pain, then rubbing it all the way to my feet and pulling it literally out of my toes.

"OK, that's it," he says, standing, "we're finished."

"Take your medicine and tomorrow you will be cured!"

I slowly stand up on my jelly legs, thank him, and take a double dose of medication for good measure. Then I crawl up to my bed on my hands and knees, and I immediately fall asleep, exhausted.

# THE ROMAN CATHOLIC CHURCH GUIDE

## TO MIRACULOUS HEALINGS

1: The disability or malady should be serious.
2: The patient should not have been improving at the time of the healing or suffering from a condition that normally might be expected to improve.
3: The patient should not have been under any orthodox treatment at the time.
4: The healing should be sudden and instantaneous.
5: The cure must be perfect and complete.
6: The cure should not occur at a time when a crisis due to natural causes has affected the patient or illness.
7: The cure must be permanent.

## RUITELÁN TO TRIACASTELA

# A MODERN MIRACLE

I OPEN MY EYES and a smile forms on my lips. I somehow feel refreshed, rejuvenated, and alive, but I daren't tempt fate.

I swing my legs out of bed and stand to attention. So far so good, and I can't feel any pain. I begin with a slow march on the spot, followed by a short stroll around the bedroom and a hop, skip, and jump.

"The pain has totally gone. I can't believe it! It's a miracle. Phone the pope. I'm cured!" I shout and break into a jolly song. I must find Luis and shake his healing hand.

Downstairs, Carlos is up early, laughing and joking with everyone, even at this unearthly hour. He points to my legs with a whisper. "All gone?"

"All gone, man." I laugh.

"Good, good," he laughs. *"Nada, nada."*

"Where's Luis?" I ask Carlos. "I've got to thank him. I still can't believe it!"

"He's still in bed," he says.

"Well, can you please thank him for me?"

"*Nada, nada,*" he says, waving me off down the road.

* * * *

So I leave the miraculous village of Ruitelán behind me with a spring in my step. I'm buzzing on life as free as a bird. There just no stopping Eddie Rock! "Yeeeehaaaaaaaar!" I'm upbeat for the first time in a long time. Maybe I should have spent a few more days in Ruitelán to see if the guys can fix the many flaws in my character.

*Oh, baby, there ain't no mountain high enough...*

Even my repetitive-song syndrome is improving.

Old farmers bid me good tidings through a shroud of Ducados smoke, and cow shit paves the way through each ancient village I traverse. Eventually, the hot sun breaks through as I finally reach my objective: O Cebreiro, ancient and sacred place. It's known as the gateway to the kingdom of Galicia, home to the city of Santiago de Compostela and the shrine of Saint James.

With miracles abounding, I sit and read about a medieval miracle that happened right here in O Cebreiro.

Legend has it that in the 14th century a peasant from the local village of Barxamaior struggled up the mountain during a terrible snowstorm to receive communion from a less than happy priest. Once inside the freezing church he scolded the peasant for his foolishness.

All of a sudden the heavy door blew open and time stood still as a warm fragrant breeze blew in around the altar. The priest and peasant stepped back in amazement as the sacramental bread and wine turned literally into the flesh and blood of Jesus Christ and thus the Miracle of O Cebreiro.

Both priest and peasant are buried in the graveyard and the Chalice is kept inside the church, encased in bulletproof glass.

I go straight to investigate the legend and leave my pack outside the door as young children play happily with an excitable little dog running around in circles. The kids tease him madly and squeal with delight each time he jumps up to lick their faces.

Inside the church I light a candle and sit for a while in the peace and quiet, renewing my vow of sobriety. I thank Saint James, Luis, and Carlos for my miraculous healing, and I feel like the luckiest man on earth, until a group of Bosch-faced pilgrims arrive to bring my miracle moment of inner peace to an end. I leave the church, and as soon as I'm outside, the little dog cocks his leg and sprays all over my pack, much to the delight of the children.

"Señor, is that your dog?" they ask me.

"Not anymore," I joke, shooing the dog away as they giggle.

* * * *

I finally feel at peace with the world. I've known nothing but pain from day one, and last night it all finally came to an end.

I spot my first-ever eagle soaring high on the thermals as free as nature intended, but peace never lasts long. I hear him long before I see him. Ahead of me is walking, talking, sea-shanty whistling, sexual octopus Steve Irwin and his handsome Fräulein. I watch in dismay as his hand slides in and out of the back of her safari shorts like he's checking the oil of his Volkswagen as he whispers sweet nothings into her ear.

Finally, I arrive in Triacastela and am immediately tempted by the Devil in the form of a German version of Benny Hill sitting and drinking a large bottle of San Miguel lager, which he offers to share with me.

I'm quite tempted, but a deal is a deal, so I show him my tablets and tell him I'm on medication.

I check in, have a shower, and find I'm sharing the disabled quarters with the man with one leg. I'm humbled again, and a bit jealous, as he has the company of the feisty German girl with the large breasts to keep his mind occupied.

In the paddock behind the hostel, fine-looking bay horses graze happily on the lush green grass. I like the idea of doing the Camino on horseback, but I couldn't stand the saddle sores and having to look after the poor animal. I've had enough trouble just looking after myself recently, but blisters on my arse, no thanks.

I go to bed early and notice the German girl sneaking into our room and sliding into bed with the one-legged chap, and in seconds she starts giggling.

# PABLO COOLIO 1; GERMANY 0

AN EPIC 9:00 A.M. LIE-IN, followed by coffee and toast in the café. I feel happy and on top of the world. "There Must Be an Angel" by the Eurythmics is playing on MTV, and I resign myself to the fact that I still have no hope in hell of mastering the Stevie Wonder harmonica solo in a million years. I could quite happily sit here all day, deep in contemplation, but the wheels of steel are already in motion. According to Swiss John's theory, these last few kilometers are where I should be reflecting and wondering how to live the final chapters of my life, but the thought of returning to Scunthorpe fills me with dread.

On the outskirts of Sarria I see the two very familiar figures of Dr. Andreas and Greta resting at a bridge. They are amazed to see me again, and the good doctor is even more amazed that I'm fully recovered. They laugh loudly as I tell the story of "the miracle at Ruitelán."

Both the good doctor and his wife look absolutely shattered.

Greta explains. "We spent the night at the monastery at Samos in a converted crypt where everybody had nightmares." She shudders.

"It's where the plague victims used to sleep," says Dr. Andreas.

"Truly horrible and now we are shattered again," she says.

I feel for both of them, and I'm pleased I stayed where I stayed, but I have to be on, so I bid farewell to my friends and hope to see them in Santiago.

As I approach the hostel in the woodland village of Ferreiros, I notice the blank, expressionless faces of ghostlike pilgrims, haunting around the entrances and exits with their worried gray faces already deciding my position in their queue. "Well, not today, José."

I give them five loud blasts of *The Great Escape* theme and a V for victory sign as I pass. Their shocked, sour faces say it all.

Rain clouds gather above me and the sky turns black, but I don't care.

I feel alive! Then, without warning, the heavens open and the cleansing, baptizing, rejuvenating rain ruins my last cigarette.

The light fades quickly as I cross the great bridge of Portomarín, with the yellow arrows leading me into a deserted hostel with no sign of life. So, cold and hungry, I trudge farther into the deserted town, sitting for a while on the steps of an empty hotel as darkness falls.

The place reminds me of a seaside resort closed down for the winter, and I can't sit here all night, so I follow my instincts and press on through the deserted streets.

I hear him before I actually see him. "Theo!" I shout.

After an eardrum-shattering, hand-crushing reintroduction, he shows me inside the hostel to the bottom bunk on the very last bed, telling me that most of the lightweight pilgrims have stayed here for another night because of the rain, creating a pilgrim backlog of miserable faces.

I manage to find a dry T-shirt at the bottom of my pack and have the pilgrim's meal at the restaurant with Alyssa, who tells me that Dave and Eva are very much an item now, staying in cheap motels and pensions instead of the pilgrims' hostels.

"They're even talking about starting a family," she says.

So on that note, I opt for an early night with Pablo Coolio. Maybe now in my sobriety I can understand what on earth he's talking about.

It might make me a better person, maybe even benefit from reading it? I climb into my damp sleeping bag and settle down for an interesting evening with Cocker's old book, but someone else has other ideas.

The man in the bunk next to mine is laid on his back with his legs in the air, farting loudly and laughing. His horrible wife on the bottom bunk next to him thinks it's funny too! The bitch.

I, however, do not think it is funny in any way, shape, or form, as a cloud of obnoxious fart gas drifts into my sleeping zone.

"Did you hear that? Ya, dat vas ein beauty!" he jokes.

"Ya, vell done, Rolf." She grins.

I knew my rehabilitation wouldn't last long.

Hatred, medieval torture, and painful death fantasies invade my once-peaceful mind. I put my earplugs up my nose and pull my sleeping bag over my head, exposing my bare legs to the damp, cold air. A deep, dark vengeance unfolds in my agitated mind, involving a large firework, a roll of duct tape, and a farting German bottom hole.

I wake up freezing in the middle of the night to a chorus of snoring and now I'm wide awake and still angry.

Pablo Coolio gives me an idea.

The industrial elastic band that once formed the cover of Cocker's prized book is now stretched tight, like a catapult, with a neatly triple-folded piece of Pablo Coolio front cover missile. Gripping it between my teeth, I take aim at the snoring German.

A couple of shots go wide. The snoring stops, and I fear my position is compromised, so I hide beneath my covers until the snoring starts again. *Vengeance is mine, said the Lord.*

*Twang!*

"ARRRRGGGGHHHH!" echoes through the darkness.

"Mich hat eine wespe gestochen" " he screams.

"Rolf, vas was dat, wat was dat?" says his wife, with her head torch on.

"Vat is happening there?" says another German.

"Rolf has been stung by a vasp!" she says.

The snoring has now stopped, and others are awake, babbling, but it was worth it. Well worth it. Pablo Coolio 1; Germany 0.

# BIRD WOMAN

THANKFULLY, THE MUNCHEN-FARTERS have gotten up early and gone. People are wondering if I've finally gone insane, as I keep bursting into hysterical fits of laughter about my silent attack. The bathroom door seems to be jammed on a stick or a pebble. So I pull it shut again and give it a good shove, shunting an elderly fool across the bathroom, and three elderly faces glare at me, waiting for an apology they are never going to get. I'd love to conduct a scientific experiment with these idiots to see why they need to block every doorway in the land. I need to brush my teeth, and one of the fools is sitting on one of the two sinks. I need to piss, and the other fool is leaning against the urinals. What the fuck is wrong with some people? I'm so angry that I manage to do all my ablutions in the one and only shower. Then I slam the door on my way out to a chorus of international abuse, as I reel off every Euro swear word I have ever learned.

Back on the trail, up ahead of me is a small woman I have seen a few times before. She has a strange birdlike face and big round glasses like Deirdre Barlow from *Coronation Street*. She even tweets and flutters nervously as I pass by. Deep down in the deepest depths of madness comes my new repetitive song:

*"Bird woman, bird woman, are you fond of dancing?"*
*"Yes sir, yes sir, I am fond of dancing!"*

I look across at her and wonder, but she's no river dancer, that's for sure. No sign of the amigos yet. Maybe I'll see Cocker and Swiss John. Tucker perhaps? Dave and Eva? Who knows?

The heavens open again and I am soaked to the bone.

In the hostel I share my small room with the bird woman and the ZZ Top look-alike I saw back in Pamplona all those weeks earlier.

My medieval buddy, Aymeric, doesn't reckon much to this section of the Camino either. He says,

> Innkeepers and servants along the road to Santiago who take pleasure in illicit gain, are inspired by the Devil himself to get into pilgrims' beds at night. Harlots who go out to meet pilgrims in wild parts between Portomarín and Palas de Rei for this purpose should not only be excommunicated, but also stripped of everything and exposed to public ridicule, after having their noses cut off.

Wow, steady on Aymeric. Meeting a harlot on route! Chance would be a fine thing, but one climbing into my bed at night, well . . . even better. But I think I would reserve his punishment fantasies for rude, farting Germans.

Eleventh-century Irish pilgrim Emmet Haggard says of this area,

I doth sallied forth, till after a couple of leagues I reached the posada of Los Gatos Negro's in a deep valley at the foot of lofty hills. Our host now demanded whether we were hungry and upon being answered "Yea" he did produce from yon larder a dozen eggs and some bacon and a gallon of wyne from't thyne bodega. While our supper did tarry, I was plyde with this finest of wyne by the finest of fair maidens and did venture forth to drink Aguardiente, a fire water most similar to our Irish poteen. Thyne host proclameth that to drink such a brew was to make thyself robust again thy powers of the local Brughas (witches) that were plentiful in these parts, upon taking heed of his words I did empty vas after vas and made merry with the maidens until I could take no more. . . . I did waketh sometime later naked and confuseth with nowt more than my pilgrims hat atop my ached head.

## SANTIAGO OR BUST!

IT'S 7:00 A.M. and sixty-nine kilometers to Santiago! What would Andy McNab do?

The thought of staying in yet another boring hostel full of farting, snoring, door-loitering, bathroom-hogging, energy-sapping Hieronymus Bosch–faced pilgrims is too much for my head to take. I just want to get it all over and done with now, get my sins forgiven, and get on with my life. Excitement spurs me on through the pines and fresh-smelling eucalyptus. After twenty or so kilometers I stop for a well-needed break at a roadside café and read a final story from my pilgrim guide.

This is what my old friend Aymeric Picaud says about this final stretch:

There is a river called "Lauamentula," because in a leafy spot along its course and two miles from Santiago, French pilgrims on their way to Santiago take off their clothes and, for the love of the Apostle, wash not only their private parts, but the dirt from their whole bodies.

Nowadays it's called Río Lavacolla, which means in Latin, *arsewash*!

I wonder what Scunthorpe means in Latin?

Two locals sit in the window seats opposite, muttering and staring as I sit down and await service. An equally grumpy little waitress appears, bringing them coffees, toast, and six minutes of babbling conversation—while I cough, hum, fidget, and sigh loudly but to no avail. She then collects their plates and disappears off the face of the earth as I wonder to myself if I have somehow attained the power of complete invisibility! She finally reappears and starts chatting again.

"Excuse," I say loudly. All three stop and stare. You could hear a pin drop, and the waitress casts me the evil eye.

*"Un coffee con leche y amón y queso bocadillo, por favor,"* I ask politely. I feel hatred burning inside them, but I've done nothing wrong. What's with these people? The sour local asks me in English if I'm a German. Then his bitter woman asks me with a hiss if I'm a tourist.

"No, I'm a pilgrim and I've come from Roncesvalles!" I tell them.

They both sit back in their chairs, pulling faces and casting sideways glances. Eventually my teeth-shattering bocadillo arrives, no doubt containing an array of pubic hair, bogies, dingleberries, and phlegm.

I can all but guess that this place has been the scene of some serious pilgrim ill behavior. Maybe the farting Germans have literally followed through here? As I leave, an Aryan-looking couple on a tandem arrives.

"*Hola, hola, buen camino,*" they say to me, momentarily happily.

I hope for their sakes they are not German. I have a little laugh to myself and continue on into a large forest, and as the day grows long, the kilometer markers are fewer and fewer. By late afternoon I've reached the village of Santa Irene and spot pilgrims of all shapes and sizes gathered around the hostel. The sight and sound of them alone spurs me ever onward.

I can't wait to see the bright lights of Santiago and feel the magic. Maybe Cocker will be there with Swiss John, doing a turn as a resident DJ in a top nightspot and gunslinging Crint Eastrood

I wonder about the nightlife, the clubs, the discos, and the sexy Galician ladies, but by 6:00 p.m. the cathedral of Santiago is still nowhere to be seen. I pass the airport and the radio station. On my left now is the Monte de Gozo pilgrims' hospital, with eight hundred free beds, looking like some kind of zombie launderette, full of dejected beings pottering around in their underpants with buckets of washing.

Their negative aura spurs me on into the city, but I still can't see the cathedral! I need to see it, touch it, and feel it.

Even my toenails are beginning to ache, and I daren't stop, even for a few minutes, as I fear my whole body will turn to stone.

Finally, the modern buildings make way for authentic medieval, and I lose the arrows for the last time. It's a quarter to ten at night, but where in the name of Saint James has this place got to?

I check into a small guesthouse and immediately head straight back out to find this cathedral, if it's the last thing I do.

THE FIELD OF STARS

# MOORE'S IRISH BAR:
# SANTIAGO DE COMPOSTELA

"WE ARE ALL MADE OF STARS," said a young hippie girl many moons ago. Well, Suzie, I made it here in the end. Saint James kept his side of the bargain, and I kept mine. The fact that I can't sit, stand, crouch, walk, or move my legs without profanity is another story altogether. As for now, I shall celebrate my success in Santiago's finest alehouses, and tomorrow morning I will have all my worldly sins forgiven at the Pilgrims' Mass, where I will place my hand into the sin elimination handy handhole and turn over a new leaf once and for all.

The Spanish version of *Big Brother* is blaring out of the television screen above my head, distracting me from my drinking. With its silly ginger-haired, ponytailed host running around like an idiot, shouting *his* head off and doing *my* head in!

But it's got me thinking . . . big brother?

Maybe the concept of spirituality is like a game of Big Brother? With Big Brother God setting the tasks and choosing who you spend your time with. When you die **/** get evicted, BBG sits you down in a big black leather chair and goes through a video diary of your entire life, starting with your first day a school right up until your very last breath. Including special guest appearances from BBS (Big Brother Satan)! With extended footage of all the bad things you've done in your life. All in front of a baying crowd, televised in heaven and in hell for all to see. In the studio audience, dead friends and relatives cheer you on while waving flags with your face on them. Finally, you climb into the elevator, and BBG poses the final Big Brother question: Will he go up. or will he go down?

*To vote up, phone 000. To vote down, phone 666. Please remember lines close at midnight. . . . Calls cost £1.50 per second.*

Either way I don't care, so I drink up and look for someplace better to go. Ten minutes later I'm sitting with a lovely pint of Guinness in a bar called Casa das Crechas behind the cathedral. The ambience is good, and I settle for a night of serious drinking in the company of several like-minded individuals and not a pilgrim in sight.

A couple of tourists pull up barstools next to me, both obviously Irish. The woman is very sexy, with that proper black Irish look about her, and her man wouldn't look out of place on *Crime Watch* or *Rogue Traders.* His chosen specialized subject would be drug running, gunrunning, or tarmacing your driveway! Maybe he got his flight mixed up with Santiago in Chile—to arrange transportation of cocaine to Ireland in Pablo

Coolio's specially converted submarine.

Or maybe they're just tourists and I've got a very vivid imagination. "Cheers! *Sláinte!*" we shout, toasting our respective futures and making our introductions. With swaying pints, Finbar tells us about the time that he shagged a trainee nun and knocked a Christian brother unconscious with a hurling stick. We clink our glasses again then Finbar proudly announces that he's also excommunicated from the Catholic Church, we all laugh and cheer.

He reminds me a lot of a workmate I once had by the name of Paddy Power. Paddy was a savage-looking Irishman if ever there was one. He had the scars of Christ tattooed on his hands and feet with his front teeth filed into vampire-like fangs. When we went for a haircut one day, the poor girl cutting Paddy's hair let out a bone-chilling scream as she shaved through the layers of wool to reveal "666" tattooed on his head. He was a rum lad to say the least, a bit like this chap.

The Irish couple drink up and leave, and I'm not far behind them.

Out in the street I smell the unmistakable scent of hashish and manage to make friends with a group of jolly Galician musicians, who offer me a well-needed toke on a large joint. My first smoke in a month.

*"Muchas gracias, amigos!"*

After a stoned stroll, I eventually find my way back to the room, and as my head hits the pillow, I'm out like a light.

The next morning rigor mortis has set solid into my whole body. Everything hurts. The only thing I dare to move are my eyelids and eyes, and even that's a struggle. I lay staring into the darkness and attempt movement, then cry out in pain as the pit bull jaws of a cramp bite down on my right calf and won't let go for what seems like an age.

After a long, hot shower, I limp into the outside world and bump into Yannick and Theo, proudly showing off their new Compostela certificates. We sit for a while on a sunny terrace with pints of Asturian cider, no longer in any hurry. Theo tells me that the Three Amigos are staying at the pilgrims' hostel not far from here, but they will soon be leaving to walk to Finisterre, so I quickly drink up and go to find them to say our last farewells.

In the army barrack–style pilgrims' hostel at the other side of town, I find the amigos being hassled by a drunken Scottish pisshead who is getting angrier and angrier by the minute. First, I think to myself, *What the hell is a Scottish pisshead doing in Santiago de Compostela?* To be honest I don't want to know, but he is hassling my amigos, and Ze looks worried. The open window behind him is a tempting option to dispatch this bum if he starts getting violent! We can always say that he fell. But thankfully, an equally inebriated Galician hobo comes into the dorm and manages to pry the drunken erbert away from my friends. We all breathe a sigh of relief as they leave noisily, with the Scotsman looking back, swearing and waving his fist.

"Why don't you come with us to Finisterre?" asks Ze.

My excuses are feeble and unworthy.

"I can see it in your eyes!" he says.

He knows and I know. . . . Ricardo takes me to one side and slips into my hand a small "Brazil" badge with the green and yellow flag. I put it on immediately and shake his hand for the last time.

I say farewell to Rodrigo and again to Ze. True pilgrims in

every way and true gentlemen. Never to be forgotten.

I make it back to the cathedral just in time for the Pilgrims' Mass and find the place packed to the rafters with tourists, pilgrims, priests, nuns, monks and druids. A few Mexican waves start but fail to take shape, and a nun sings "Ave Maria" as the priests file in and begin mass. A group of men in cassocks undo some thick, heavy ropes and any minute now the bells will ring and we can all leave. Instead, they lower down a World Cup replica and set it swinging right through the central isle of the cathedral, bellowing out frankincense and myrrh as a group of Japanese tourists get dangerously camera happy.

"Health and Safety Act 1974" comes to mind, or possibly "Not now, Mr. Yamamoto."

Thankfully, the procedure takes place, with no fatalities or serious injuries, and at the end of the ceremony we all hug and shake hands with our fellow pilgrims and head back out into the sun.

Next on my agenda is to get my Compostela certificate and last, but not least, find a travel agent. The certificate was easy enough to obtain, but trying to find a flight into the UK is proving to be a difficult and costly business.

"You could fly via Amsterdam," suggests the helpful travel agent.

And so the story ends where it started . . . Amsterdam!

"Hello, is that Señor Gilberto the Moor slayer?"

"Eddie, me old lad. How the hell are ya?"

"I'm flying in tomorrow afternoon," I tell him. "What are you up to?"

"It's my birthday on Saturday: the big forty," he says excitedly.

I've known Gilbert three years and have been to two of his

fortieth birthdays already, so I suppose one more won't hurt, will it? Will it?

So the next day I'm sitting in the sun, at the bar, waiting for my taxi, and a grim realization hits me like a ton of bricks. "Shit. I never put my hand in the handy handhole to have my sins forgiven! Fuck!"

There's still time. I leave my pack with the barman and sprint back to the cathedral as the morning mass is in full swing.

I sneak in through a side entrance, but the forgive-me-not handhole is cordoned off with a security barrier and a guard in place. The clockwork South African girl sees me and begins frantically waving at me from the pews, blowing my cover, and I realize that it's now or never! As the smoking silverware flies through the air; I slip under the barrier unnoticed and stick my fingers in a well-worn hole. Then I'm immediately escorted off the premises by an angry nun.

*"Ir romero y volver ramera."*

*"Go a pilgrim, return a whore."*

One of the oldest recorded sayings of the pilgrimage.

# WHAT EDDIE DID NEXT

WELL, AS YOU GATHERED from the last chapter of the book, I flew straight from Santiago to Barcelona and then back to Amsterdam. From there I took a train back to Rotterdam to meet up with my aforementioned short fused former comrade, Señor Gilberto, to help him celebrate his third fortieth birthday. A happy Birthday it was not. Drug fueled drunkenness ensued ending in the usual bloodshed. This time it was Gilbert who came off the worst after being given a special gift of 67 stitches by a knife wielding maniac. I proceeded to the airport the next day with my tail between my legs and back to England to face the music. It was during these troubled times I began writing this book and gradually my life improved. But in 2011 I had had enough of living in England once and for all. So I sold everything except for my tools and my van and came back to

Galicia with the intention of buying and restoring a ruined house on the Camino, But the Lord moves in mysterious ways.

In 2012 I bought an abandoned farmhouse deep in the Ribiera sacra region of Galicia very close to the *winter* route of the Camino de Santiago. My new intention was to build a writers retreat and try to live in peace but as always temptation and trouble were lurking just around the corner.

### 2018-01-04

Well Jesus went into the wilderness for 40 days and 40 nights. Buddah Shakamoonie managed a whole 7 years and I'm not far behind him. Ghengis Khan would be proud as I have spent most of this time living in a Mongolian Yurt even in the Galician winter. Also during these hard times Karma caught up with me and valuable lessons have been learned the hard way.

While living here in Galicia I have met a whole cast of interesting people from Nuns to Narco traffickers. Witches and Warlocks, Fools and Fiends to say the least. From the comfort of my half finished wooden cabin I have began writing again. My first project is *Be Careful What You Wish For,* a book about my 7 years of adventure here in Galicia. I am also writing a comedy script featuring some of these strange characters. As they say life is stranger than fiction.

People often ask me *'Did the Camino change your life in anyway?'*

What do you think?

# REFERENCES

"To Be a Pilgrim," John Bunyan, 1684.

*A Practical Guide for Pilgrims: The Road to Santiago*, 8th edition, Millán Bravo Lozano, 1998.

*Liber Peregrinations*, Aymeric Picaud, published in the year 1130.

"Wish You Were Here," Pink Floyd, 1975.

"Jesse" Joshua Kadison, 1994.

"Old Woman, Old Woman," Trevor and Simon (swing your pants).

*The Waltons* theme tune, Jerry Goldsmith, 1929.

*The Great Escape* theme tune, 1963.

"Waltzing Matilda," Banjo Paterson, 1903.

"He Ain't Heavy, He's My Brother," the Hollies, 1969.

# REFERENCES

"Dirty Old Town," Ewan MacColl, 1949.

"Little Donkey," Eric Boswell, circa 1959.

"Walking Back to Happiness," Helen Shapiro, 1969.

"Highway to Hell," AC/DC, 1979.

"Walk This Way," Aerosmith, 1975.

"St. Elmo's Fire," John Parr, 1985.

"Catch Me if You Can," Brendan Shine, circa 1970s.

"Ain't No Mountain High Enough," Ashford & Simpson, 1967.

"There Must Be an Angel," Eurythmics, 1985.

*The A-Team* theme tune, Mike Post and Pete Carpenter, 1983.

"Walk Like an Egyptian," the Bangles, 1986.

"Road to Hell," Chris Rea, 1989.

"Loco in Acapulco," the Four Tops, 1988.

"Bette Davis Eyes," Kim Carnes, 1981.

"Peaceful Easy Feeling," the Eagles, 1972.

"Seven Drunken Nights," the Dubliners, 1967.

"Every Breath You Take," the Police, 1983.

"Piano Man," Billy Joel, 1973.

"Chirpy Chirpy Cheep Cheep," Middle of the Road, 1970.

# ACKNOWLEDGMENTS

I WOULD LIKE TO THANK the following people for their support: Sir Jack Herer, God, Suzie, Jamie, Paul, Sarrel, and Alex. The Mule, Mr. John Lydon, my old English teacher. The Devil. Nick and Helen, Dale and Emma, Ridley and Erin. Becky P., Ralph K., Simon B., Cocker and Swiss John. Buddah Shakamoonie. The Three Amigos. Harriet S. John and Mike. Gilbert. Steve P. Jo and Noel. Pokie and Klausie. Martin T. Andrea J. The spirited people of Spain and some of my fellow pilgrims, and last but not least, Mary Magdalene, the patron saint of sinners, and Saint James for getting me there in one piece.

CPSIA information can be obtained
at www.ICGtesting.com
Printed in the USA
LVHW04s0405180518
577492LV00002B/5/P